Praise for Gl

"In a world that often feels like it's lost its shine, Katie illuminates the path to finding the glow-worthiness in each of us. She helps us rekindle the light within that allows us to glow with the peace, energy, purpose, and love we crave and deserve. There has never been a more important time for us to learn how to ignite this inner glow so we can live the radiant lives we deserve, and help those around us do the same. *Glow-Worthy* is a trustworthy guide for modern times, and for the ages."

—Nicole Beurkens, PhD, licensed psychologist and author of *Life Will Get Better*

"In an overwhelming and shaming world, it is all too easy to lose our natural glow. It begins early, and before we know it, we can't even remember what it was like to feel glowful and alive. In *Glow-Worthy*, Katie Silcox calls us home to our radiant nature. She reminds us of our inherent luminosity and gifts us the tools and practices that we need to restore it. This magnificent book is a lighthouse of divine possibility for anyone ready to come back to light. If it doesn't help you glow, then let it go."

—Jeff Brown, author of *Hearticulations* and *An Uncommon Bond*

"*Glow-Worthy* is 100% worth your time and energy. In this real-life, laying-it-all-out-there approach, Katie brings vulnerability to a new level, helping the reader understand that they are not alone in their feelings, that there IS HOPE for growth, and that it's okay to slide backward. She offers an authentic way to help us all redefine ourselves and our spiritual relationships. I laughed out loud when I read in chapter 2 that while in the ER her doc told her to consider, yep you guessed it: meditation! Katie is a rockstar; read her book!"

—Michael J Breus, PhD DABSM, author of *Good Night, The Sleep Doctor's Diet, The Power of When,* and *Energize*

"*Glow-Worthy* is like a warm, sweet cup of tea—it physically feels good to read this book. Katie has brought forward her warmth and humanity combined with thought-provoking ideas, real practices, and helpful information to create a refreshing new lens for how we show up in the world."

—Amy Stanton, author of *The Feminine Revolution* and founder and CEO of Stanton & Company

"*Glow-Worthy* is a love song to your soul and a skillful guide to welcoming, reclaiming, and honoring *all* of yourself. Sourced from the depths of embodied wisdom, a relationship with the sacred, and personal truth, Katie skillfully weaves rituals, practices, and science to amplify our access to self-nourishment, presence, and love."

—Tracee Stanley, author of *Radiant Rest* and *The Luminous Self*

"We live in a time obsessed with the mind. We are so busy optimizing, hacking, grinding. We've lost touch with the Soul. The word God has become taboo. Katie, in her sweet, light-hearted, down-to-earth, and most authentic way, shines a light where it needs right now to be shined: deep in our hearts where the spirit of God whispers ever so gently. Katie's spiritual journey is one I can relate to. A full circle heroine's quest we all need to hear right now!"

"*Glow-Worthy* is the perfect antidote for the times when your inner glow starts to fade and the clear mirror of your Soul clouds over with doubts. Sharing wisdom born of years of self-inquiry through scientific research, ancient yoga traditions, and deep practice, Katie Silcox offers advice and practical tools to help you reconnect with your Divine essence, realign with your Soul's purpose, and truly shine your light in the world."

"As a neuroscientist, I am often asked to evaluate books on topics related to the mind-body connection and personal growth. After reading *Glow-Worthy* by Katie Silcox, I am excited to say that this book is truly exceptional. It seamlessly blends ancient spiritual practices with modern scientific research to offer practical tools for awakening our inner light and cultivating self-love. One of the key messages of this book is that each of us has a unique inner light that, when nurtured, can radiate out into the world and heal those around us. As a scientist, I appreciate how Katie cites studies that demonstrate how our energy and presence can influence those around us. But as a human being, I am moved by her message that we each have the power to make a positive impact in the world simply by sharing our light. Throughout the book, Katie offers a variety of practices for cultivating self-love and nurturing our inner light, including movement, meditation, and gratitude. What I appreciate most about her approach is that it is both accessible and customizable. Whether you are new to spiritual practices or a seasoned practitioner, there is something in this book for you. In short, I highly recommend *Glow-Worthy* to anyone looking to deepen their connection to themselves and to the world around them. By embracing our own brokenness and celebrating our beauty and sacredness, we can truly transform ourselves and the world we live in."

"This book is an apothecary of rich teachings distilled straight from the stars and Katie's own deep experiences as a woman, leader, change maker, and passionate voice for secular and nonsecular alike. Thank you, Katie, for writing this beautiful, updated 'book of hours' for the modern soul. For those of us willing and ready to do the work, it inspires us to overcome our blocks to the wild perfection of our own inherent nature. Katie's intellectual prowess and southern-belle grace is literary nectar. Not only are we encouraged to remember our stories and integrate our parts, but her words and the practices she has curated lead us directly to what this book promises—feeling the worth and infrangible strength of our gorgeous, timeless spirit."

"Katie Silcox is one of our most important messengers, with a supportive and healing guide for women that is accessible, deeply resonant, and needed more than ever. *Glow-Worthy* is an owner's manual for the human heart and soul that will give readers the freedom and healthy entitlement to go after the dreams that had previously been elusive or even concealed. It will be a welcome path for so many."

—**Michael Fishman, founder and leader of Consumer Health Summit**

"*Glow-Worthy* is a must-read for anyone seeking to connect with their inner light and embrace their sacred imperfections. Katie Silcox offers a refreshing approach to spirituality that is relatable, inspiring, and empowering. I loved every page of this book and can't wait to share it with my community!"

—**Lisa Marie Rankin, author of *The Goddess Solution: Practical Wisdom for Everyday Life***

"*Glow-Worthy* guides you to the freedom to be beautifully human through conscious life experience. Using these tools, the full expression of life becomes available to you. With kindness, compassion, and love, this book guides you into the freedom to radiate and to be."

—**Myra Lewin, founder of Hale Pule Ayurveda and author of *Freedom in Your Relationship with Food***

"A powerful reminder of the light within each of us waiting to glow from the inside out. Katie is honest, magical, and genuine about the truth within all of us. After reading this book, everything will glow—yourself especially."

—**Dr. Keiko Finnegan and Dr. Sera Sheppard, founders of Kinfolk Optimal Living**

"It is so easy to want to throw in the towel many days, yet Katie reminds us that it is so close, that it is already within us, we just need to give it some energy. Katie is like a best friend and cheerleader showing us the way through ancient teachings, her own personal experience, and clear practices. You are worthy, and when you recognize that, you will glow."

—**Hub Knott, author of *Living Nature Connected* and cofounder of The Living Earth School**

"*Glow-Worthy* reminds each of us that change is inevitable and that our choices determine the direction of that change. In this book, Katie shares wisdom gleaned from decades of study and growth and presents this in a way that is both relatable and accessible. Employing the practices in the book—contemplations, reflections, meditations, and new and different actions taken in daily life will, no doubt, bring the reader to a state of Glow that they hadn't previously encountered and allow them to shine that light for others."

—**Mary Thompson, Ayurvedic practitioner, educator, and consultant**

Glow-Worthy

Also by Katie Silcox

Healthy, Happy, Sexy: Ayurveda Wisdom for Modern Women

Glow-Worthy

Practices for Awakening
Your Inner Light and
Loving Yourself as You Are—
Broken, Beautiful, and Sacred

KATIE SILCOX

BenBella Books, Inc.
Dallas, TX

BenBella Books, Inc.
10440 N. Central Expressway
Suite 800
Dallas, TX 75231
benbellabooks.com
Send feedback to feedback@benbellabooks.com

BenBella is a federally registered trademark.

Printed in the United States of America
10 9 8 7 6 5 4 3 2 1

Library of Congress Control Number: 2023007747
ISBN 9781637743720 (trade paperback)
ISBN 9781637743737 (electronic)

Editing by Leah Wilson and Leah Baxter
Copyediting by Karen Wise
Proofreading by Isabelle Rubio and Jenny Bridges
Text design and composition by PerfecType, Nashville, TN
Cover design by Brigid Pearson
Cover image © Shutterstock / Martin Ferriz
Printed by Lake Book Manufacturing

Special discounts for bulk sales are available. Please contact bulkorders@benbellabooks.com.

This book is dedicated to all the bodhisattvas, from India to Appalachia (known and more often unknown), who taught the only thing that ever really heals any of us: *loving presence*. And to Cristal Mortensen—Queen of Black Point—who is probably one of them.

CONTENTS

PART 1
Foundational Glow

1

Beginnings

You hold in your hands a book that has the capacity to awaken a connection to the sacred inside you. Not because I am a special genius who has cracked the spiritual code, but because there is Divinity inside your body. Right now. Untapped.

You may be thinking, *Wait, did I read that correctly? Is this woman telling me she's going to teach me how to connect to God? Through my body?*

Yes. Yes, I am.

I'm telling you that it's possible to live from a place of deep connection to something that is far sweeter, far more powerful, and far wiser than you ever knew.

To feel aligned in your mind and heart with a sense of purpose that resonates all the way to your soul.

To establish a direct line to a source of wisdom that will guide you throughout your life.

And to recapture an authentic relationship to the aliveness within your physical, breathing body, which in turn can deepen your connection to your soul—your unique inner embodiment of the Divine.

This book can help you come home to a forgotten truth—that you are, in this moment, deserving of standing in the fullness of who you are. You deserve to glow.

What exactly do I mean by *glow*? Is it about radiant skin? That new shimmering golden body serum? A sexy vibe? Well, all of those things are okay— but true glow comes from recognizing our sacred nature. *Our inner light is what makes us glow.* And that glow isn't something you earn. It is here now in abundance. You're already worthy of it—just as you are. This book will help you access that inner light in order to get that real-deal glow.

Your glow comes out when you start holding *all of you and your life* as sacred ground—as holy. You will have more trust in your intuitive power. You will be able to speak your boldest truth from a place of steadiness and compassion. You will have a deeper capacity to work through the inevitable pain and discomfort that arise when we take an authentically spiritual approach to living. You will be able to love the most hidden, shameful parts of yourself. You will also be able to tap into the collective wisdom of your ancestral line, helping you heal past familial wounds that dampen the clarity of your light. You will have a deeper knowledge of that part of you that is both unique and deeply connected to the bigger matrix of life. When we are walking in our glow, we feel deeply connected to the most authentic and vibrant parts of ourselves: love, healthy sensuality, wisdom, willpower, forgiveness, boundaries, and true self-esteem.

It's important to emphasize that awakening our glow is *not* about becoming something else. You already are glow-worthy. But if you are anything like me, you forget it sometimes (or a lot of the time). In a way, you can think of what this book asks you to do as a subtraction process. Nothing is added. Everything is simply remembered, as we take away some of the old beliefs and habits that block our perception. I'll repeat it again: The glow is in you right now.

We can also think of this inner glowing as *real holiness*—a place where every part of you is welcome to the spiritual party.

How do I stand behind such a bold statement? Because after over two decades of deep spiritual scholarship and personal practice, as well as nearly that long sharing and teaching women the same, I am ever more convinced of one thing: Given enough time and space plus some practical tools, all people are primed to both recognize and receive guidance and comfort from their spiritual source, whatever name they give it.

I'm also living it.

I am not perfect or enlightened—sometimes I'm still a hot mess—but I have experienced that inner glow, which feels like endless compassion. When I pause and put my hand on my heart, I find the intrinsic worth that has been there all along. I know who I am beyond my struggles. I love myself more than ever and experience a confidence that can only come from finding a place of refuge within myself. I have gone down deep into my own darkness and come out on the other side more whole, loving, and settled into the truth of who I really am. In the words of writer Anne Lamott, I've had moments in my life that "would make Jesus want to drink gin straight out of the cat dish," and I have used those moments of pure fire to first melt and then forge me into the woman I am today.

You have probably been there, too—the health issues, the loneliness, the bad breakup, the feeling of being stuck in a job, the anxiety and addiction, the selling random shit on eBay to pay rent. Sometimes the drama of life makes you lose faith in your basic goodness, or even the goodness of a Divine Creator.

I lost both.

At the height of an enviable career as an in-demand yoga teacher and published author, I found myself in a Virginia emergency room, head on my mama's lap, afraid I was dying. The month before I had been featured—skin-tight hot-pink leggings and slicked-back platinum blonde hair—on the cover of the world's best-known yoga magazine. When the ER doctor said that I was "just" having an anxiety attack, he prescribed me Lorazepam—and then kindly suggested I consider taking up meditation and yoga.

Humble pie, meet Katie Silcox.

It was a wake-up call that made me question all the "healthy" and "spiritual" things I'd been doing and get real about finding what actually worked.

Central to this healing path was reclaiming my spiritual life. From a young age, I deeply longed for a sense of greater connection to the Divine. I was, and still am, highly sensitive. I always felt things strongly—often, it seemed, more strongly than others did. I could even feel the feelings of people around me. It was confusing a lot of the time. Overwhelm was a constant companion.

I also grew up Southern Baptist in the 1980s. My entire childhood was like a low-key Christian revival, with my family attending church three times a week and doing church-related activities in between. There was a lot of hellfire and sexual guilt. I struggled to understand why, according to the church, I couldn't love this world and all of the beautiful and wonderful things it held, and also love God. Or why people who didn't believe what we did wouldn't be "saved."

But there was also sweetness that came from church life: a real community, a sense of morality, and a deep knowledge that God loved me.

These disconnected messages and feelings left me totally confused about my religion and myself, especially as I got older.

Like many teenage girls, I struggled with body image, disordered eating, and my own overwhelming emotions. Overeating became a private ritual that, in the moment, gave me a sense of control. I also sought attention from men and became addicted to the temporary thrill of outer validation.

Anxiety and panic attacks in my early twenties led me to yoga. I'd abandoned the faith of my youth when I went to college, and I felt this ancient system from a faraway land was somehow truer to who I was.

Most of all, yoga gave me a formula to follow: *Do this pose, eat this way, chant this Sanskrit mantra, and hold your breath for this long, and you will feel better—AND rediscover God, but without all that judgment.*

For a while, yoga worked. Really well, in fact.

But inside, something was still unsettled. And that "something" is what eventually landed me in that Virginia emergency room. It would take me years to understand and unwind all that led up to that moment, which I still think of as one of my darkest days. But my biggest lesson—and heartbreak, if I'm honest—was the realization that yoga and meditation alone couldn't solve my problems.

I believed that food, men, and gurus had all the answers, but they'd become like Band-Aids on hidden wounds that actually needed light and air and tears to heal.

That fateful day in the emergency room was a critical turning point in my life. It led me to let go of the rigid yoga and meditation doctrine I'd been following for years, and instead get serious about studying why my nervous system seemed to be working against me.

I worked with compassionate experts who helped me access the frozen, terrified, and angry parts of myself that yoga and meditation were temporarily keeping at bay.

It was not fun.

I also went back to my roots and began exploring my family lineage. I reconnected to the Christian traditions I remembered from childhood that *did* feel beautiful, especially the prayers, hymns, and loving words of Jesus Christ. I also studied and worked with the energies of Mother Mary, Sophia, and Mary Magdalene, the feminine counterparts to Christ who were so sorely lacking in my Baptist upbringing.

I embarked upon a spiritual healing journey, drawing upon traditions near and far as I spelunked my own inner consciousness. I worked with therapists who specialized in somatic trauma processing, Jungian psychology, early-attachment repatterning, and energy work. I realized that I was a part of a growing revival of neglected but powerful wise-woman traditions. It felt like coming home.

I stopped traveling as much. I took a hiatus from men—both dating and projecting my power and my pain onto gurus.

And I made the quest to forge an authentic connection to my own version of God, the cornerstone of my life.

Today, I am happy to say that I feel more at home in my body than I ever have. I also know that my physical body is *not* my only refuge. I sleep pretty well most days. I love myself in a more tender, real way than I ever knew possible. But most importantly, I feel a continuity of spiritual connection that is independent of the inevitable ups and down in my *very* human life.

I've also been teaching other women everything I've learned through my online health-coaching platform, The Shakti School. In collaboration with women's health experts from both folk medicine and functional medicine perspectives, I've designed programs to help as many women as possible reclaim their power and heal themselves.

But my struggle to understand my inner life isn't what this book is about. *This book is for and about you.*

In its pages, you will be given the best information, embodied practices, and proven tools I've discovered on my journey. From Tantra yoga to modern trauma-release methods, from Ayurveda to the latest research on the science of happiness, from traditional women's wisdom to an updated take on mystical Christianity, from modern neuroscience to energy work, I want to share with you what has deeply supported me, and what I have seen work for thousands of other women through The Shakti School. I think you will find these practices simple yet profound. Easy and embodied. All in the service of your own deep intuition.

WHAT IS "HOLY," REALLY?

Before, I mentioned this word: *holy*. The practices you will receive here rest on a radical premise: *That your true inner glow comes from realizing that every part of you is holy—and that no matter what is going on in your life, you are worthy of that glow right here and now.* Yes, every part of your life has the capacity to be infused with holiness. And I get that you may have a weird relationship with the word *holy*. This book is designed to take you into the deeper meaning of the word, *not the religious meaning*, that points to a holistic way of being in relationship to your soul.

One of my favorite definitions of the word *holy* comes from the Dutch and German root *heilig*, meaning "whole and complete." Another comes from the Old English *halig* meaning "something that is consecrated and sacred." This implies a capacity to hold everything about you as worthy of existing. It has nothing to do with being sanctimonious or "good." It's not about purifying all of your negative thoughts and feelings. Holiness is revealed within us when we take every aspect of our experience as workable and worthy.

Can you imagine that? Genuinely feeling like you were tapping into something sacred when you could embrace all of you? That is what I hope this book can help you discover. And perhaps more importantly, I hope this book will help you *live* from that place more and more.

So often an authentic spiritual connection requires a deep homecoming to the granularity of everyday life. Imagine driving to your next blind date feeling totally whole and loved from deep within. Imagine offering a presentation at work from a genuine sense of confidence, no matter the outcome. Imagine feeling the divine in your actual body instead of just repeating the words of "love your body"/"body positive" culture. Imagine feeling your anger without immediately feeling ashamed of it and pushing it away. Imagine going through a life crisis, disease, or death with a clear sense that something sacred is alive and present in you, even in the darkest of moments.

That is what living in holiness is all about: *perceiving the glow that is already given.*

Maybe you are thinking, *OK, but what does it even mean to connect to God? And why should I have that as a goal? And ew yuck, I can't even stand the word* God!

It may seem obvious, but so much of our collective story as women is that we must constantly be working, earning, achieving, or beautifying something in order to prove our worthiness and finally get happiness. When we are more spiritually connected from within, this constant achievement delusion starts to slowly melt away. As we try less and learn to receive more, we experience a type of spiritual joy that no amount of succeeding at work, marrying the right person, or beautifying our bodies can ever provide.

Looking back at my own journey, I now realize that I was desperately looking for someone else to tell me how to heal. I felt that if I could just get the right practice, the right mantra, the right yoga sequence, the right breathwork, the right diet, the right therapist, *then* I would be able to feel at home with myself. Through the process of doing all of these things and studying with so many great teachers (and some less-than-great ones), I realized that my glow was inside me all along.

Don't get me wrong. I am a *big* fan of teachers and mentors. But what I found was that the best teachers taught me how to connect to my own body, its subtle energy, and its ever-evolving wisdom. This inner wisdom led me to my own true spirituality, something no one could ever take from me.

I can't predict how this journey will go for you, but what I can promise you is that I've seen these tools and techniques work for thousands of women in my trainings and my year-long Ayurveda program. I have watched decades of pain open up and melt away in the light of these practices. I have watched women unfold into their softness and stand in their firmness. I have also watched self-proclaimed "type-A alpha women" weep tears of relief when they finally realized they could release the tight grip they held on their lives and lean into that inner softness they had neglected while trying to stay afloat in a sea of "getting it all done perfectly." I have watched women craft their own spiritual lives and reap the real-world benefits. But mostly, I've watched the hardened parts of my own heart soften and begin to heal.

This path shows us how every heavy, painful, shameful thing we carry inside is the fuel that forges us into what we can become. It's about how our old stories, patterns, and wounds (and—spoiler!—those of our culture, too) keep us from being as happy and living as fully as we can. It's about how inside every woman resides an intuitive healer, a fiercely loving mother, a sexy vixen, and a wise and unshakable ally to guide, nurture, and protect us at any and every stage of our lives.

What would it look like if women got back in the driver's seat of their spiritual lives? Let's face it, we've been told over thousands of years how to pray, meditate, and be with God based largely on the opinions of men. And don't get me wrong, I love men, especially the wise ones. But it is time to step out of the church pews and into the pulpits of our own individual spiritual lives.

You might say it's our birthright. The very things that make us human— our natural bodies, our capacity for compassion, the fullness of our emotion and intuition—are dowsing rods for spiritual guidance. We are meant to *glow*!

Most of us just need a little guidance. And my hope is that this book gives you permission to craft an adaptable framework for your own journey to know God—or Goddess, spirit, the Tao, enlightenment, Universal Love, whatever you choose to call it.

The practices in this book are what worked for me, and what I continue to follow every day.

Today I think of myself as a Zen Buddhist, nature-loving, energy-worker woman who prays daily to Jesus (who also wears high heels, eats hamburgers, and listens to hip-hop music). And I've written exactly the kind of guide I wish I'd had. Something that would have helped me know that who I am—who *we* are, at our core—is Love itself.

After reading these pages, I hope you will leave with a sense that:

You are an inherently spiritual being who is on this Earth to do great things.

You don't need to bend and conform to any belief system to earn your way into God's love.

You, exactly as you are, sins and scars included, are holy.

You glow.

THE ROOTS OF THE GLOW-WORTHY APPROACH

This book's roots are informed by over two decades of study and practice in many realms, including (but not limited to):

Perennial mysticism from a vast array of sources and my own direct experience. This book also holds channeled women's wisdom based on my more than two decades of devout studentship, scholarship, and teaching of yogic and Ayurvedic traditions, mysticism, and depth psychology.

Nature. Systems such as Ayurveda, Druidism, Taoism, and Shamanic Animism see a deep connection between our health and our connection to our truest heart. They also see nature as the great teacher and master regulator. In this book, we will lean into this approach—to not only God as a universal consciousness or force, but *God(dess) as a teacher* within the natural world that moves through us as a glowing energy or life-force.

Modern Science, especially that which is related to the nervous system, trauma, and emerging research on the physiological benefits of love and compassion. We will also explore some emerging neuroscience around happiness, joy, and gratitude and what having a spiritual life does to our brains and bodies, as well as the relationship between our biology and the experience of spirituality.

Tantra/Buddhism. This includes not only traditional Hindu and Buddhist Tantra and Ayurveda (which I have a master's degree in and have actively practiced for twenty years), but also Tantra in the largest sense of the definition. Tantra is not about mind-blowing sex, as we often mistakenly think in the West (although yay for mind-blowing sex!). It's a way of expanding our awareness into *knowing who we really are*—the Divinity that lives within—while at the same time fully enjoying this temporal human life in a way that contributes to that divine knowing.

Think of Tantra as inner-glow training 101. It is a time-tested method of working with your thoughts, energy, and emotions in a way that alchemizes. That means we take all of who you are, the good and the bad, and we transform it into holiness. Think of Tantra as the mother of metaphysical bonfires, the one that takes all the gunk you have—the hard stuff, the ugly stuff, the stuff that makes you feel alone and flawed and totally unlovable—and transforms it, leaving only the pure ash that is left when all that pain is removed: You, as in, The Real You, at your truest and most perfectly imperfect and beautiful nature.

Mentorship. Mentorship has been one of the core ways I have learned in this lifetime. This book was written during an intensive mentorship period of four years with a brilliant therapist named Cristal Mortensen, to whom this book is dedicated. So much of my evolving understanding of trauma healing, energy work, and spiritual life has been influenced by my direct relationship to her. Multiple energy-based practices

I share with you in this book are ones that I have done with her. Needless to say, I am really grateful to have her in my life. You can find out more about her work in the resources section of this book. In the acknowledgments section, I also mention many of the other teachers and mentors with whom I have had the privilege (and sometimes pain) of working with. I encourage you, dear reader, to take these practices, integrate them, and make them your own—embody them and then feel free to evolve them, translate them, and share them as well.

THE G-WORD: A NOTE ON SPIRITUAL TERMINOLOGY

It has been my experience working with thousands of women that any time we bring up the topics of our bodies, our emotions, and our *deepest* (even unspoken) desires, things get sticky very quickly. That is even more true when I bring up the topic of God, religion, or spirituality. We all want a more spiritual life, but the words and topics associated with spirituality may also conjure discomfort.

When I use words like *God, Goddess, spirit, soul, religion, spirituality, the sacred,* and *Divinity,* I invite you to reconsider your relationship to these words. I know that they may bring up your past and that may invoke powerful feelings. For many of us, the word *God* may touch something angry or tender, with vast numbers of us feeling like spiritual orphans within a religious tradition that betrayed us.

You have every right to feel let down by religion. Many of us may also feel let down by the spirituality of our recent ancestors. And I completely get that (more on my story with religion to come).

It's also possible that your past religious connection just needs an update, *where you get to be more you.* If any of the words I use in this book for Divinity feel uncomfortable to you, I encourage you to explore the deeper "why." If it is unbearable to use the word, *let it go.* Find another word or way of connecting that feels right to you. It has to feel real. But sometimes, the words that make us the most uncomfortable may be pointing to an aspect of our spirituality that needs healing.

For example, for years I avoided the word *God.* I was mad at God and everything my ancestral Christian religion represented. I wanted the Goddess!

So, I chucked God out the window and dove into everything Divine Feminine I could get my hands on. Every time I heard "God," I would cringe. It would take me back to the Bible Belt South and all the hellfire guilt of my childhood, and I would throw up a wall.

Connecting to the idea of a female Divinity was deeply healing to me as a woman, and it opened me up to a totally new realm of possibility within my spiritual life. But I was out of balance. Over time, I realized that my own relationship to the masculine needed healing. For so many women, including me, it can be incredibly healing to invite in a masculine divine presence that will never betray or abandon us. In this book, we will explore a 360-degree spiritual life—up and down, in and out, masculine and feminine. It's all here.

Reading this book may bring up feelings and sensations that are uncomfortable. This is to be expected and even encouraged. But it is my hope that by the end of this book you have a different relationship with spirituality—and a different relationship with "spiritual words," reclaiming and redefining them, evolving and elevating them.

On this journey together, we will enter into a relationship with the deepest parts of ourselves, which are often the places that store the most pain. As you do this work, especially if you have experienced trauma in your past or in your community, it can be incredibly helpful to work with a counselor, coach, or therapist. I will provide some great references in the back of the book that may be of use to you on your journey.

Most importantly, this book is *not* about me telling you how to connect to God. It's about *you* discovering an authentic connection on your own. As you read, don't be in a hurry. You can take your time with this book. If something doesn't feel right now, it may feel right a few months or years down the road. It also may never feel right, and that's okay too.

HOW TO READ THIS BOOK

This book is not necessarily meant to be read in a linear way. I do, however, recommend reading the *Foundational Glow* section first, as it forms the basis of the Glow-Worthy philosophy and includes practices that are perennial (meaning they keep popping up!) as you move into a deeper relationship with yourself. We will also work with some root concepts in these chapters that are initiation points on the path—the base from which we begin all other practices.

The book is divided into three main sections. In the first section, *Foundational Glow*, we will explore the core ideas and practices of this book—holiness, presence, love, and life-force energy. In the second section, *Finding Your Inner Light*, we will learn how to hone our intuition, work with soul-loss, and open our hearts to our core wounds and limitations. In the last section, *Bringing Your Glow to Life*, we will bring these glow-strengthening practices into our relationships, sexuality, rituals, and celebrations. We will also learn how to cultivate and protect our glow as we move through this complicated, messy thing called life.

This book will (lovingly) nudge you not just to read the words on the pages, but to actually pursue a direct experience of the concepts inside. It will push you toward the embodied, immediate experience of your own energy, emotions, and intuitions. In fact, this book holds the idea that it is only this unique, embodied, direct experience that can lead you to insights, truths, emotional releases, and soul awakenings.

That's why this book is also chock-full of embodied, energy-based presence practices, including both prompts for journaling and some of the very meditation practices I have used for over twenty years. (The meditation practices have also been recorded for you and will be available at theshaktischool .com/glow-worthy-meditations/.) I encourage you to contemplate, write things down, and pause to feel. I will also give you some great rituals, tools, tips, and self-care techniques (including a few from my close friends and mentors). There is also a resource section at the end of the book for further study, support, and therapeutics in many forms.

Take notes on the things that feel the most important or interesting to you so that you can come back to them. This book is a reading journey meant to inspire you and remind you of your soul! But it is also part practice manual, meant to be returned to as needed.

As you read, you may find that there are certain practices within the chapters that you are drawn to right now. Do those! And there may be others that you are less attracted to and want to save for later or never do at all. Connecting to your authentic spirituality is not a one-time project or a box you check in your daily to-do list—it's an ongoing journey. Think of this as a process-oriented approach, more than a final-goal kinda thing. Rather than using the practices to find a place of perfect spiritual peace and equanimity, or as a way to escape your emotions, I recommend thinking of the approach as a new way of lovingly orienting to your own mind and your life. In this way, everything is allowed and *we can open to what is already given.*

Lastly, the path toward remembering your glow is neither straight nor always clear. Many times, spiritual life feels like two steps forward, one miserable step back. Living from the soul involves a constant pulsation. Some days it expands out and we feel open and in alignment with our soul's bigger purpose. Other days, it contracts and we feel lost in the wilderness of our past compulsions, addictions, and old mental patterns. During those contractions of spiritual life, you may feel like you've lost your way, or that you're worse off than when you started and less connected to your soul than ever. Please know that these times of Divine contraction are just as important as the feel-good expansions. In fact, it is often during these moments—when we feel like a hot mess and God is hiding from us—that our soul is being honed for some greater expansion. A bigger glow. Stay the course.

2

Broken

I was born in the 1980s in the little Virginia mountain town of Abingdon, on the Tennessee border. I grew up with all things Bible Belt: country hills, country music, and country churches. And since I was from God country, the church played a massive role in my life. The Fellowship Chapel, where my family worshiped, called itself nondenominational, but in practice, it was very Baptist. And very Southern. We were taught that the Bible is the inspired Word of God, is infallible, and can be taken literally.

Satan, or the devil, is a very real thing for Baptists, and he provides continual temptations and stumbling blocks for the Christian. The most important tenet in my church was that the only way to be "saved" and go to Heaven (and to avoid Hell and Satan) is through baptism, when you ask Jesus to come into your heart.

As the script of every Sunday went when I was a little girl:

You were born a sinner.

Your flesh is evil.

Come up to the front of the church.

There you will find a man in a suit.

He will tell you the secret prayer—the initiation rite that will bring you into safety, into salvation.

Repeat after me.

And you will be saved.

I *really* wanted to be a good Christian, and I remember being very excited to be baptized when I was seven. I stood in my white robe in the tiny water tank hidden behind the plastic potted plants on the pulpit, I felt our pastor Lester's firm hand on the middle of my back. I felt like I was getting married to Jesus.

"Katie, do you now trust in Jesus Christ alone for the forgiveness of your sins and the fulfillment of all God's promises to you? Are you ready for eternal life as you forsake evil and turn to Jesus? Do you intend with God's help to obey Jesus's teaching and follow him as your Lord and Savior for the rest of your life?"

"I do," I said earnestly.

"Now, Katie, as you have proclaimed your faith in Jesus Christ as your personal Lord and Savior and in obedience to his command, I now baptize you in the name of the Father and of the Son and of the Holy Spirit."

During sermons, I'd sit with my little girl sit-bones pushing down, spine straight, perched like a good listener who wanted an A in class. I'd hold my small pink Bible, the one Lester gave me at birth that had my name written on the inside cover in my mama's cursive. I also remember Lester's kindness, humor, and fatherly guidance toward our little family. He was a father figure to my own fatherless dad, and would show up in "just the right moments" to check on my young parents. I remember him speaking something he called "French" to me, and I just thought that was the most amazing thing I'd ever heard in my life.

Lester would also preach about the need to differentiate the flesh—and all the worldly things it represented—from the spirit. The things of this world would never make you happy, he assured us, and they blocked what really mattered: God's love.

In the church of my youth, the choice was clear: Jesus or sin. Love for God or love for the world. Despite my love for Jesus, it was always a hard sell for me, sensitive creature that I was. I held to both things strongly: the world and my spirit.

Back then, family life was synonymous with church life. We went every Wednesday and Saturday night, and on Sundays, three times: in the morning, at lunch, and again at night. And while there were many great things I got from being a part of a church community, it didn't help me manage one of the hardest things anyone can go through: being a young girl.

I left childhood with something of an identity crisis, common for young women. In my early teens, my emotions felt so big. Life was a roller coaster of feelings that I didn't know how to manage or understand. And so I turned to food to soothe myself, establishing an eating disorder by the time I was thirteen that would take years to unwind from my psyche.

The church never helped me address this. Our youth group sessions only fueled teenage angst, with Krispy Kreme doughnuts, Christian emo rock, and horror stories about damnation and Hell. On top of this, the church told me that my passionate, fiery nature was wrong. That my love of the world, my desires, and the creativity they ignited were sinful. Even worse, the church taught me that my sexuality, my body, and my basic female nature were all sinful. I even signed a promise card at age thirteen, swearing off sex until marriage. As a result, I felt fundamentally broken. I learned to turn these big emotions inward, telling myself that I was flawed and fat and that there was something bad about me.

By the time I went to college, I rejected my religion. I was determined to find a spiritual path that felt more aligned with my spirit. Like so many spiritual "orphans," I turned to the Eastern practices of yoga and meditation. The lessons learned from my childhood spent in church, where I was told that love of God and love of this world were incompatible, I let go. From the East, I was offered a vastly expanded understanding of the human experience, one that said our divine nature isn't separate from material reality, but rather infused into every particle of it.

I also found a highly developed method for working with my mind. Beside my bed was a stack of books on Eastern philosophy and mysticism: *The Tibetan Book of the Dead*, Ram Dass's *Be Here Now*, BKS Iyengar's *Light on Yoga*, and Paramahansa Yogananda's *Autobiography of a Yogi*, among others.

I traveled to the holy places of the Eastern mystics, yearning to know any technique available for freeing myself from the deep suffering within—an emotional longing the source of which I struggled to put my finger on and a sense of anxiety that followed me wherever I went.

In my quest, I spun with Sufis on the beaches of Goa, prayed with yogis on the banks of the Ganga River, and meditated in silence for days with Buddhists in the mountains of Ladakh. It was in India that I met Indra and A. G. Mohan, the elder students of the famed Krishnamacharya, the man credited with bringing hatha yoga to the world. They became my yoga and Ayurveda mentors and, with great tenderness and compassion, they taught me the yogic basics of knowing God, including their vast insight into the ancient Hindu texts the *Yoga Sutras*, the *Hatha Yoga Pradipika*, the *Upanishads*, and the *Yoga Yajnavalkya*. It was through working with them that I developed my lifelong love for Ayurvedic medicine, a holistic health approach that co-emerged alongside spiritual life in India.

While Buddhism and yoga helped calm my mind, I still felt something was amiss. Many of these teachings emphasized developing an egoless state beyond the "monkey mind"—the constant chatter of our always-seeking, always-analyzing human brains—through a non-attachment to desire, the senses, and worldly pleasures. Over time, I began to question why knowing God meant denying everything that made me human: My heart. My desires. My full spectrum of emotions. My longing to experience life in Technicolor, with my senses and creativity and sexuality engaged and celebrated.

In some ways, the messages from those Eastern holy men (and they were almost always men) differed little from the messages I had received growing up in the evangelical Baptist church. Only back then the ego was called "Devil," and we kept it at bay by praying to Jesus instead of emptying our minds.

Could a spiritual path really coexist alongside the things that felt most natural and important to me?

Sometimes I even harbored the secret belief that I was a forgotten priestess. Somewhere within, I knew I could use my sexual energy wisely, to heal and creatively inspire. I was as comfortable concocting herbal remedies and dancing under the moonlight as I was sitting in Lotus Pose diving into the infinite silence of my consciousness. But there was nothing in the Christianity that I had grown up with that supported the idea of a nature-loving priestess-God-woman—and there was little in the male-dominated yoga world reflecting this either.

I began to wonder: In the history of religious and spiritual systems, *where were all the voices of women?*

If they existed, they didn't seem to have written any books or codified many practices. Maybe their writings were intentionally suppressed. Or maybe they were just too busy healing people, having babies, and getting shit done.

I didn't know what to believe back then, but in my heart I knew that there was something more than just the surface experience of being alive. That there was an energetic force that connects all living things, and that I was a part of some greater, kinder intelligence. More and more, I intuited that there was something uniquely feminine about this intelligence. That this authentic-to-me spirituality and the feminine energy were intimately connected. Not that it wasn't also available to men. It was available to everyone! But we had all denied it for a really long time.

I also suspected that the very conditions of our human experience—the things that make our hearts sing or break, the experiences that make us grow, our relationships with others, our connection to nature—were actually . . . *holy*.

Simply stated, I longed for a spiritual orientation that would allow for divinity to *coexist* with my flaws, and that had room for my emotions and other more subtle energies and intuitions. I longed for a spirituality that was based in Carl Jung's longing: "I would rather be whole than good."

Then I discovered Tantra, a system that stems from Hinduism and offers a spiritual framework that holds all of life as sacred. It is both a philosophical approach and a method for getting rid of the obstacles, both inner and outer, that keep us from knowing who we really are and accessing our greatest potential. Tantra also maintains that it's possible to attain spiritual liberation while still living and enjoying the world. Through it, I began to glimpse the possibility of my tender humanness actually *being* the vehicle for establishing an unshakable connection with the Divine.

I spent the next decade studying, practicing, and teaching within this system.

It's important for me to say this: Today I don't consider myself a Hindu, a religious Christian, a Tantrik, a yogi, or as belonging to any particular religious organization or formal lineage tradition. While I reference some religious and spiritual traditions throughout the book, these frameworks are just useful maps to access your inner glow. They are no replacement for your own life's wisdom. Saying that, I deeply bow to the traditions I have studied and incorporate many elements of them into my daily life and practices. I am a true believer that individual spiritual evolution and innovation *can and must* coexist with the ancient wisdom from the past.

Instead, my spirituality is 100 percent unique and 100 percent mine. On some days I pick up the words of Buddhist teacher Thich Nhat Hanh. On others, I act like a Dionysian priestess who heals through love-filled sex. Some days I fall at the feet of Jesus Christ. Other days, I am completely surrendered to the magic of energy work and the way my breath and body can return me to the arms of the Earth.

And while I haven't figured everything out (and probably never will), I have learned a framework for remembering that I am worthy of being in my glow, here and now. And that is what I will share with you next.

3

Holy

It is impossible to awaken an embodied connection to the glow inside us when we are still at war with parts of ourselves. I'm all too familiar with my capacity to throw some parts of me out of *The Garden of What Is Acceptable to Love.*

This chapter will walk you through what may be a missing ingredient in creating your authentic spiritual life: the radical idea that *all of you holds intrinsic holiness.* And that it is often the most difficult, scary parts of ourselves that reveal our glowing, already-worthy self underneath.

At the heart of this idea is the understanding that the messiness of our daily lives (emotions, relationships, our bodies) is holy ground for spiritual revelation. It's a belief shared by many mystical traditions (and may be a forgotten root of religious traditions). But it wasn't what I was taught. I learned that my passion was wrong, I was inherently sinful, and I needed to be saved.

No one told me that my body was a Divine temple housing a holy and sacred spirit. That my emotions were my connection to my humanity. That my desires and dreams and even my insecurities were aspects of my holiness. And perhaps most importantly, that my vulnerability was a portal into my light, my real self, my glow.

It took decades of study, practice, and even teaching to finally understand that *all of me* wasn't just *useful* on the path to find authentic spirituality—all of me was *required*. You see, you aren't only lovable when you are righteous and kind. You are lovable as the angry, spoiled brat that you sometimes are. You are lovable as the scared child. You are lovable as the lusty sex kitten. And the way to begin this practice? You take whatever it is you are holding in your heart and mind and *that* becomes the sacred soil to till.

Many of the tenets and practices within the "holy framework" I offer here are actually thousands of years old, but they are as relevant today as they were back then. And in my view, returning to the essence of these older traditions has the potential to provide a bridge for the modern woman to the deeper meaning she longs for in her life. We can move from some of the pains of modern culture—namely disconnection and dishonoring the inner feminine—to belonging and acceptance of the deep complexity of who we are. As you continue reading, it may be helpful to remember that the ancient core essence of religious and spiritual teachings may be drastically different from the manifestations we see today.

It's as if a bad telephone game has occurred, where the original mystical messages of someone like a Christ or Buddha have been misinterpreted (or completely altered!) by humans possessed by their own egoic power games and projections. Returning to our own body, our own being, helps course-correct these flawed messages. As we access our own inner spiritual compass, we can understand the words of our mystical ancestors in their essence. In this way, we own our spiritual life, and we become transmitters of an embodied, more alive form of spirituality.

Embracing all of life as holy is mysticism for the woman who wants it all: spiritual freedom, worldly success on her own terms, a loving romantic partnership, and a deeply authentic inner life. This chapter will give you the basics of one particularly salient ancient tradition from India called Tantra, which subscribes to the idea of a holy animism within all things. This tradition allows you to awaken to your true inner glow, not only on a meditation cushion, but while living your daily, messy life.

We can think of Tantra as a spiritual approach indigenous to the subcontinent of India. Within Tantra are complex traditions, gods, goddesses, rites, and rituals. We can also think of it more broadly, as a fundamentally human, universal approach to *using the entirety of who you are (hello, holy!)* as a portal into freedom from your small, limited sense of self *(hello, ego!)*. For the purposes of this book, we will approach Tantra not in a scholarly sense, but in the more universal sense of letting *presence* be our spiritual North Star and *love* our inner compass.

(I'll also make the case that many mystic systems, philosophies, and religions come from a similar Tantra-like root. More on that later.)

WHAT TANTRA IS—AND WHAT IT'S NOT

Tantra is widely misunderstood by Westerners as a sexual practice. In fact, Tantra is misunderstood everywhere. In the East, where it originates, some fear that Tantra is *only* a form of black magic with rituals involving human skulls and meditating on dead bodies! In the US, perhaps because of our puritanical origins, Tantra is seen (as popularized by the musician Sting) as sex that lasts for days.

As exciting as this sounds (I mean, who doesn't want a sex marathon?), Tantra is not just about better sex. It is a system of rites and rituals, exercises for the body and mind, and philosophies designed to help us move beyond our limitations. The goal of the practice is to cultivate spiritual liberation, and along the way access the full potential of our individual capacity to be of unique service in the world.

The word itself is descriptive: In Sanskrit, a classical language of South Asia and the sacred language of Hinduism and Buddhism, *tan* means "to stretch" or "to expand," and *tra* means "a device for" or "practice of." Its root, *trayatire*, means "freedom" or "liberation." And so, a *tantra* is a means through which we are expanded out of limitations and liberated into knowing who we really are, beyond the inner voice of the mind that we have confused with our "real self."

Another definition of *tantra* is "to be touched deeply in the heart." Yet another is "a loom," alluding to the capacity we develop to weave spirituality into our daily life.

Perhaps the most important element of this system, and what greatly appeals to me, is the belief that the most human and imperfect aspects of our nature—our handicaps, disadvantages, self-defeating beliefs, even our worst tendencies—are tools to use toward that liberation. Instead of denying our limitations, or labeling them as "bad," Tantra encourages you to bring what ya got, so to speak, as fuel for the fire of your own personal journey.

We'll spend much more time with this, but for now, I hope you feel—as I did—a sense of relief that this path doesn't ask you to be someone else. Your whole self glows, flaws and lusty longings included.

✳✳ A GLOW-WORTHY CONTEMPLATION ✳✳
The Garden of What Is Acceptable to Love

*What are the parts of myself and my life I have kicked
out of the Garden of What Is Acceptable to Love?*

What are the parts of me that don't feel wanted and holy?

What are the parts of me that do feel glowing?

*What are some of the conditionings and false beliefs I have
received from my own religious or spiritual upbringing?*

What in me or about my life may be in need of spiritual repair?

One of Tantra's organizing principles is that there is a primary feminine power, called *Shakti*, that animates all things, from rocks to humans. This feminine force is something the Tantric path holds in common with many mystic traditions, but it was systematically removed from many of the religious traditions we practice today.

Yes, you read that correctly: The feminine was systematically removed from religion. This has created an imbalance of spirit that harms the souls of both women and men of so many faiths. In order to feel whole—to feel holy— we need a balance of both feminine and masculine within.

When we speak of *feminine* and *masculine* here, we're speaking not of gender, but of universal archetypes. There is no perfect definition of these archetypes. In fact, a part of the beauty of the concept is that you learn to intuit and experience them for yourself. But the feminine is traditionally associated with nurturance, creativity, spontaneity, love—qualities all humans posses.

By removing this feminine force from our religions, we have essentially sucked the animating principle out of everything. And when we aren't able to see the sacred quality in all of life, we can treat people, nature, animals, and even our own bodies as worthless and meaningless. A spiritual tradition without the sacred feminine becomes a lifeless ritual, destined to be overtaken by consumerism, greed, power plays, and politics.

In the Christian tradition Shakti is known as Sophia. In the mystical Judaic practice of Kabbalah, she is known as Shekhinah. This feminine force is expressed in our bodies through *prana*, or life energy (also called *chi* or *qi*). Prana is inherently creative. You could even think of it as sexual. Not in a "let's get it on" kinda way, but in a life-bringing, life-affirming, constantly replicating and renewing kinda way. And this creative force, according to Tantra, *is* the driving power in our human lives, urging us along. "Birth yourself! Birth creative projects! Birth babies! Birth ideas! Evolve!" it urges.

Can you imagine going to a church, synagogue, or mosque where the service began by honoring the spirit of creative, sexual life that lives in all things? Imagine the priest, rabbi, or imam addressing the congregation with a full-spirited: "How's everyone's sacred life-force awareness this morning?"

This is *exactly* what we would do in a shrine that honored all of life as holy.

You see, life wants us to create things. It truly is our nature. (In fact, studies show that people who have no creative pursuits or sense of purpose often feel depressed.) We can even use our development of this creative energy to connect even more deeply to our inner light, as well as to something bigger than us. Creative energy is the fuel of spiritual life—and as we'll see later on, in chapter six on energy, our physiology thrives when we have it.

Tantra teaches that because life is inherently creative (that is, always birthing new things), living fully means pursuing your passions. Feed those parts of you that want to grow. Be as big in this lifetime as you can be. This even extends to worldly success, an idea antithetical to many religious and spiritual traditions, which see meekness and poverty as requisite for spiritual attainment.

If something is part of the fullest expression of *you*, Tantra says, it is spiritual. Seeking and attaining what you truly desire, in your heart, is living in alignment with God, with the Divine force within you. Our job as humans is to align ourselves with that infinite source, our highest potential, and then to express that potential through our words, thoughts, and actions in the world. We will learn to separate what we *really want* (love, belonging, and connection) from what we *think we want or have been conditioned to want* (perfection, more material stuff, job titles, and money, to name a few).

There is another aspect of Tantra that, when I learned it, made me sit up in my seat: the celebration of the feminine in all her forms.

Her body.

Her mind.

Her heart and emotions.

Of course! I remember thinking when I learned this. It just made sense.

It was also an important moment for my relationship with God. I struggled for so long with the notion of a strict, judgmental God that you had to appease to stay in His/Her good graces. But I could totally get behind the idea of a God complemented by the Divine Feminine, a powerful creative and nurturing force that could be as fierce and directional as it was warm and welcoming.

And while, of course, the essence of divinity has no gender, it felt incredibly healing to view my feminine expressive qualities—my emotions, my creativity, my passion, even my curvy body that I'd battled for as long as I could remember—as sacred and powerful.

DREAM BIGGER

If God had a billboard She wanted you to see every day, it might say, "Dream bigger, honey." We are so much more powerful, loving, and wise than we know. And our lives are so much more vast than the myopic conscious our ego can fathom. Remember, the nature of your mind is pure peace. The nature of your heart is pure love. Take that in for a minute.

With this in mind, rather than *What's wrong with me?* the question then becomes: *How can I free myself from the inner confines that hold me back from true wisdom, pure consciousness, and the fullest expression of this human life?*

To help you start dreaming bigger, here are ten principles that will kick-start your journey into remembering your glow-worthy, Shakti-filled self. We will dive deeper into these as we continue along this journey together, but for now, how about trying them on for size?

Ten Principles for Remembering Your Glow

Glow-Worthy Principle #1: It's okay to want things.

You were wanted by the Divine! You are here because God *longed* for you to be here. Desire is a part of reality, so it makes sense that you have desire, too.

Glow-Worthy Principle #2: You are a mirror of God.

God is peace and love. The nature of your mind (behind your thoughts) is peace. The nature of your heart (behind your emotions) is love.

Glow-Worthy Principle #3: You need not give up the pleasures of the world to have a spiritual life.

You are allowed to get enlightened and still like sex and chocolate. The Tantriks encourage us to experience not just *moksha* (spiritual freedom and non-attachment to the temporary things of our world), but also *bhoga* (the sensuality of being in the world and enjoying nice things) and *bhukti* (the attainment of worldly successes and accomplishments).

Glow-Worthy Principle #4: The wound is the way.

You can *alchemize* your real (and perceived) limitations. Each of us was born into a particular set of life circumstances that dramatically affect our lived experience of the world. Many of us know the feeling of being held back, and in some cases deeply harmed, by family dynamics, sociocultural inequities, our genetics, or even our astrology. We may struggle with body-image issues, mental health challenges, sexual abuse, and class/race-based trauma. And while it is important to do our best to right these wrongs on a social, psychological, and developmental level, on a spiritual level, our past pain can be an entry point into our connection to the sacred. The deepest wounds hold both the poison and the medicine. We will explore this principle later in the book.

Glow-Worthy Principle #5: All of life can be spiritual fuel.

Anything in your life can be used as a spiritual tool *if it works to get you closer to your goal*. And you are the one who decides what your goal is.

Glow-Worthy Principle #6: Everything in the universe exists inside you.

Microcosm = Macrocosm. If you are experiencing challenges, you are also equal to the task of overcoming them and fully equipped with every power in the cosmos and nature to support you in doing so.

Glow-Worthy Principle #7: Holy living means holding the tension of the opposites.

Psychologist Carl Jung spoke of the importance of being able to hold the tension of the opposites in our journey to knowing our true selves. On this journey, we may feel like we are hitting up against paradoxes. Our world trains us to see things as good and bad, black and white. And sometimes that is necessary for daily life, but the deeper spiritual quest inside asks us to see *nuance*. Here are some examples: We are both interconnected with everything and deeply individual human beings. We are both totally alone and never alone. We need help, but at the end of the day the path to our spiritual individuation is a solo job. We don't need to stay in bad relationships or jobs, but we can also learn a lot from them about the deeper reasons we may have been drawn to them in the first place.

Spirituality does not make us islands of isolation. When we are living from our wholeness, we can feel both our independence and our deep relationality with others. Unlike the view of nature as a resource to be used solely for human consumption and progress, living within holiness requires we understand that we are all part of a web of interconnection and interbeing. When we touch one aspect of the web, we touch all of it. When we destroy or abuse a part of the interconnection, that creates a downriver effect on other things. We are also only able to positively affect this vast matrix through *becoming* the changes we want in this world.

Glow-Worthy Principle #8: Everything is alive.

Everything we perceive is full of God. Plants, animals, rocks, and humans (and even our thoughts and feelings) are all alive and therefore sacred. All the material world is honored as an expression of a divine force as holy as any human.

Glow-Worthy Principle #9: Your body holds your teacher.

See your body-mind as the container for your inner teacher. Your relationship to the sacred doesn't need to pass through the lens of any one individual, culture, or even religious tradition, though these can certainly help guide you. *Your body* (which holds the psyche) is a direct communicator with the realm of holiness. Think of it as a temple that holds category-breaking mystical medicine.

Glow-Worthy Principle #10: Your life matters.

This human life has a bigger meaning than punching a time clock, buying shit on Amazon, or looking young for as long as possible. You are here to glow! Just like an acorn holds the information it requires to become a mighty oak, you are the carrier of a holy soul-blueprint, unique to you, that has the capacity to help you become who you are meant to be. Not in Heaven. Right here, on Earth. Holy Little You.

4

Presence

There is a part of your being that doesn't need a New Year's resolution. It doesn't need to lose weight, find the right partner, get a great job, or heal from heartbreak. It doesn't even need this (or any!) book.

This part of us is called *presence*. It is both always available and often hard to find. It is both the beginning and the ending place for everything we do in this book.

Presence is a rare gem in our ever-more-distracted world. To be present in the modern era can feel like a Herculean effort. Our smartphones are constant attention grabbers, offering up a temporary distraction from boredom, irritation, loneliness, and any other feeling we'd rather not be having.

But we are here in this world together. And we are called to the task of presence if we want to live a more authentic, glowing life. In fact, presence is the first step in the deeper practices in this book. Without presence, all hope of finding our inner light is futile. With presence, we allow all things to be as they are. This is the realm of the holy, remember?

So, what is this magic spirit serum we call *presence*?

At its most basic, presence simply connotes existence, or being. We can also understand presence as existence with intent. I think of presence as a willingness to be in the moment with whatever it is we are feeling, sensing, and observing, both inside ourselves and outside.

Just like compassion, presence as a practice within global spiritual traditions is almost universal. In fact, presence is the essence of all forms of meditation. Judaism, Zen Buddhism, Hinduism, Taoism, and even Christian contemplation practices remind us of the deep value in bringing our minds and hearts to the now. It's as if presence is a doorway into the heart of the Divine inside. According to one of my mentors, Cristal Mortensen, presence is actually a *requirement* for Divine connection.

Presence is ridiculously simple. But it can be unbelievably hard to achieve. Especially when what we are seeing or feeling is absolutely *yuck*.

THE MAGIC FORMULA FOR REMEMBERING OUR GLOW

Presence is the pathway to glow. And after twenty years of study and practice, I am ever more convinced of one thing: that there is something alchemical and downright magical about combining presence with the intention of love (which is why these are the first two important practice chapters of the book).

I have distilled it down to a formula:

 PRESENCE + LOVE = THE REALEST, MOST CONNECTED YOU (aka MAXIMUM GLOW)

If we could become truly adept at working with presence and love, everything else would be almost unnecessary. In fact, all the other things we are attempting to understand and work with throughout this book are just methods that help us get to more presence and love. We could even think of any spiritual method as a way of removing the things that are keeping us from presence and love.

The equation of PRESENCE + LOVE can be applied to any moment in our lives. But let me repeat, being present and holding the intention of being loving (to self and others) is absolutely one of the hardest things I've ever learned to do. It is so much easier to focus on our thoughts, stories, and other mind distractors. But the more we engage it as practice, the more it can spontaneously operate in our lives.

Love is the secret sauce in the presence equation, and we will go deeper into that in the next chapter. For now, though, let's really focus on presence.

WHY PRESENCE IS HARD

Presence is the willingness to be with whatever is occurring, irrespective of whether we like it or not. And I don't want to sugarcoat this: Being present can be tough. When we are present with ourselves, and with the world outside, our minds may notice the things we don't like and the feelings we have been working really hard to avoid for a long time. You see, presence is a quality of mind where *we are with what is.* It is the continual returning of your attentional laser to what's actually real, to what's actually happening.

There is often a misunderstanding around meditation that we sit down to meditate and automatically "find calm." We think that the practice of being awake and aware will suddenly make us feel better.

It has been my experience that quite often the opposite is the case. When we become fully present, we are made witness to everything that's been sitting underneath the surface. And that's a lot to handle! That is why we do it in small amounts, chipping away every day at our inner world, until one day, we can hold all of ourselves. This is why it can also be helpful to have a teacher, mentor, therapist, or guide to help us navigate the content that arises as a result of being present. If we feel that what arises is past the threshold of what we can deal with alone, we should make sure to seek out that kind of support.

The more we cultivate presence, the more we develop access to the part of us that is brave enough to respond calmly and consciously to the feeling of being hurt, angry, or scared inside. We all carry with us old mental impressions from our pasts (aka baggage). These impressions are supercharged with emotion and lead us to react in specific ways. In turn, those reactive thoughts create more feelings. And thus the cycle of emotional reactivity continues.

In the moment, our moods and thoughts may seem very real, important, and justified. Often this is because we are rehashing an old story from the past that acts as a filter on everything we see and experience in the present. While sometimes our thoughts and feelings are accurate reflections of the current moment, most of the time they are shaped by a buildup from the past. Presence is the dissolving serum for that old filter. It allows us to see ourselves and our lives with clear eyes.

WHY WE SHOULD PRACTICE PRESENCE
(EVEN THOUGH IT'S HARD!)

Presence brings us deep. It helps us grow the muscle of being fully awake and aware in the reality of the world and ourselves. Presence is high-level spiritual badassery. It is both the starting point and the endgame in the journey of you realizing who the heck you really are (which is more awesome than you can ever fathom).

One of my favorite ways of entering into a relationship with presence comes from Thich Nhat Hanh. He teaches us that we can enter presence by simply saying to ourselves: "Darling, I am here for you." He says that if you are truly present, this mantra will produce a miracle: You become real. Becoming real means living from your most authentic self rather than behind the masks and personas we build up over the years.

Presence is a digestive enzyme for the pain of your past. It acts as both a guide through and a softening serum on old patterns, enabling us to see ourselves and the world *as they are now* and not all of that old gunk from long ago. Presence is the thing that allows us to pause when we want to react with repetitive, hurtful behaviors. It also teaches us how to process the things we are great at running from.

Presence slows down time. Ironically, as we become more present in the flow of chronological time, the possibility of another form of time opens up to us. Many people who practice being present describe having a different relationship to time, whereby we enter into an eternal experience of time, rather than a linear "getting" from one moment to the next. By becoming fully present, we connect to a sense of something sacred that is timeless. This sense may also show up as a deeper feeling of connection, belonging, love, or wisdom.

Presence is relationship gold. The ability to be present makes you a better friend, parent, lover, and co-worker. It is also the channel through which we can achieve deeper levels of relationship. As we are more present with ourselves, it becomes natural to be more present with others. And we all know how good it feels to be with someone who is deeply present with us.

Lastly, presence is spiritual gold. It is at the root of becoming a heartful human. The thinking mind speaks in the language of the intellect through words and concepts. Presence speaks in the language of the heart. It involves all aspects of you—thoughts, sensations, emotions, the five senses of perception, and, yes, subtle spiritual qualities (like the ability to sense and work with energy and intuition) that are virtually impossible to feel if we are distracted.

The Franciscan Sisters of Mary say that "spirituality is heart knowledge." We can think of presence as the portal through which we can access this heart knowledge. When we live there, we live from the truest version of *what our heart wants and knows.*

When we are present, we can hear the quiet whisper of our heart, speaking through its own vibration. And we know the heart is speaking when we feel it. For me, when my heart speaks, it is as if suddenly, for a moment in time, all my sense of loneliness melts away. My isolation disappears, and I know, from the deepest place I can know, that I am never alone.

PRESENCE IS IN THE BODY

One of the best ways to become more present is to come home to the body. You see, it's hard to feel at home on the planet—to feel that we belong—when we do not feel at home inside our own bodies. We each *have* a body, but how much do we *live* in that body, in the present moment?

Sometimes it's tough to feel like we belong inside our own skin. It's easy to push the "eject button" and leave our bodies through overthinking, overdoing, and under-feeling. Understandably, there are times when we need a temporary reprieve from the depth of feelings swirling inside us. That's okay. It can be hard to stay with ourselves.

But the idea of this chapter is that with time and care, we can learn to return to our home and to belong to ourselves a little more each day.

When we are living in our thoughts, we are often in the past or in the future. Our body lives in the present. When we live in the realm of thought, we often end up feeling estranged from our body and less than fully *here*. That said, our thoughts aren't the enemy. Sometimes it's helpful to think about the past and plan for the future. But we need to give the body and mind some time to come together in the present. This is one of the great gifts of meditation. Through practicing meditation, our presence begins to slowly dissolve the old stories and reasons why our spirit might find it hard to stay inside the body. This is called *embodied presence*.

PRESENCE IS NATURALLY EMBODYING

What does it mean to be embodied? It can be challenging to define with words, as the body speaks through the nonverbal immediacy of feeling. You see, we each have our own sense of what it is like to be inside ourselves, inside the world. This feeling comes through the unique experience of our own individual body—sensations, vibrations—and our subsequent interpretations.

When we bring our awareness to our body, we may feel varying sensations: tingling, constriction, openness, aliveness, pulsation, cloudiness. We may feel a warm, pulsing honey flowing down our arms and legs and throughout our torso and face—like we are being rocked inside ourselves. We may also just kinda feel like shit.

It's all allowed—and welcomed—in embodied presence. Slowly, with practice, we grow our ability to be in the full spectrum of our experience and not seek distraction. We learn to trust that all of us—emotions, thoughts, inner feelings, the sensory realm of taste, touch, smell, sight, and sound, as well as our observances of the world outside the body—is welcome and digested.

YOUR MIND IS COMPLEX

Presence has another big benefit besides embodiment: It allows us to become aware of more and more subtle layers of our own mind. Through practice, we become aware that the thing we call "me" or "my mind" is vastly complex. It may help to think of your mind as having different parts. Just like your body has different organs, your mind has its own anatomy.

The part of our mind we most often identify with is our conscious narrative. This is the endless running commentary we create about our life, what we like, what we dislike. This mental flow seems to have an agenda of its own and it is astoundingly adept at crafting stories about reality and making strong judgments about people (including ourselves!).

This ongoing commentary is largely based on our commentary from yesterday, the day before that, and the day before that, ad infinitum. The flow of this steady stream eventually builds momentum. In this light, it's easy to see how we can get stuck in old mental patterns about who we are, who others are, and what possibilities exist in our future. When we identify with the more conversational, "thinking thoughts" part of our mind, we run the risk of confusing our inner narrative with the totality of who we are.

Another part of our mind is the subconscious. Think of this as a storehouse full of all of our past experiences and memories. These are the thoughts and feelings that we don't consciously use every day. It would be really hard if we were consciously lugging that stuff around all day long, so our psyche pushes it down underneath our conscious mind until it's overtly triggered—or until we go deep diving into our own mind, which is what we often do when we meditate.

Even though we aren't aware of what's going on in our subconscious, it still drives much of our experiences and ways of seeing the world. It's the source of many of the motivations, impulses, and reactions driving that conscious commentary on the top surface of our mind.

Yeah, I know. It's a lot to think about. And let's not even get into the collective unconscious—which is a realm where our mind is connected to everyone else's mind, past and future!

But here is the good news: We have another part of our mind that is free from all of this. It's the highest aspect of our mind. In the yoga and Ayurveda traditions, we refer to this part as *buddhi*, which comes from the same root as the word *Buddha*.

This higher aspect of mind, the true Self, is like a really great inner compass. Think of it as your highest-level conscience. It knows what's best for you and what you should probably avoid. It is untouched by both the constant narrative on the surface of your mind and your subconscious emotions and past experiences. (We will get more into this part of our mind later when we discuss its important role in our intuition.)

Lastly, there is an aspect of our mind that is pure consciousness itself. It's the part of you that's aware of all the other parts of you. And all the great teachers say the same thing—that pure consciousness is the magic doorway into inner freedom and the holy glow we all long for. And it's accessed through presence.

So with that, let's dig into some presence practice.

PRACTICAL PRESENCE

You can start to cultivate more presence right here, right now, with whatever you've got going on. It doesn't matter if your heart is breaking or if you are in the hospital fighting an illness. It doesn't matter if you're struggling with addiction or if you are on cloud nine on your honeymoon with your dream lover. All of us can start being present right now.

Let's end this chapter with an actual *practice* in presence. Whether you practice being present with this or any other meditation, entering into the present moment lays the foundation for all the chapters to come.

And when in doubt, remember the formula:

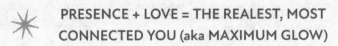

PRESENCE + LOVE = THE REALEST, MOST CONNECTED YOU (aka MAXIMUM GLOW)

✦ A GLOW-WORTHY MEDITATION ✦
I Am Here and I Can Stay

Feel free to read these meditative scripts through to get the general idea, and then practice them on your own. I also recommend recording them in your own voice on your smartphone and listening to them while meditating. I have also created a free augmented audio version of each of the meditations, which you can download at theshaktischool .com/glow-worthy-meditations/.

Take a moment to remind yourself that you deserve to take a pause in your life.

You deserve to relax into your own presence, no matter what state you find yourself in. No matter what is going on in the outer world.

Now, feel the contact between your body and the chair or floor.

Feel the weight of your body, feel gravity like a gift, pulling you down into this moment. Here and now.

Become attuned to your breath. Notice the rise and fall of the inhale and exhale.

Feel the gentle pause at the top of the inhale and bottom of the exhale.

Follow every millimeter of the breath. As if it mattered. As if it were enough.

As you relax deeper and deeper into accepting every aspect of this moment, inner and outer, say to yourself, silently or aloud: I am here. And I can stay.

Let your eyes soften and become even more receptive. I am here. And I can stay.

Let your heart soften and become even more receptive. I am here. And I can stay.

Let your belly soften and become even more
receptive. I am here. And I can stay.

Now become present to the sensation of air on your skin. Is it
cool or warm? Is there a breeze? Simply notice the skin and the
sensation there. Be totally present to your skin. Let your skin soften
and become even more receptive. I am here. And I can stay.

Now be present with the stream of thoughts or images in your mind. Try
not to consider any thoughts bad or wrong. Just be with them. Let your
mind soften and become even more receptive. I am here. And I can stay.

Now notice any feelings, moods, or emotions. Without labeling them as bad
or good, simply notice them. Notice also how both the thoughts and emotions
shift and change. Notice how it all shifts and changes. Let your emotional
being soften and become even more receptive. I am here. And I can stay.

As you practice, notice that there is something that remains. It rests behind it
all. It is the part of you that has been noticing. There is an aspect of you that
was watching the thoughts, emotions, sensations, and skin and body feelings.

It is aware. It is a witness. It holds an unwavering
commitment to just be with you.

You to you—in all of your beautiful and broken parts, all of your
wanted and unwanted parts. This presence is behind the persona
that you present to the world, as well as the scared little girl inside
of you that is ashamed, angry, or afraid and wants to hide.

Feel this presence more and more, like a massive ocean that can hold
all of the waves of all of your parts. Become more identified with this
presence than all the other parts. This part of you is always okay. It is
ancient and forever new. It's been with you since the moment you took
your first breath and it will be with you at the moment of death. Rest
in this presence, remembering the mantra: I am here. I can stay.

5

Love

"**B**eloved, let us love one another, for love is from God; and everyone who loves is born of God and knows God. The one who does not love does not know God, for God is love." (1 John 4:7–8)

Many spiritual traditions claim that there is a deep connection between Divinity and love. If we take that as a central soul-truth, it makes sense that a lot of our spiritual practice would revolve around two things: cultivating love intentionally and removing the barriers built up against our natural state of lovingness. This requires an extreme amount of willingness to be present with ourselves, which is why we started the practical aspects of the book with our winning formula:

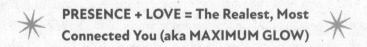

PRESENCE + LOVE = The Realest, Most Connected You (aka MAXIMUM GLOW)

Something magical happens when we can connect with our hearts and allow ourselves to feel loved by something bigger than us. We can think of this "something bigger" as Divine Love. This universal love, or love of God, can be thought of as *pure* love. This love doesn't care about your imperfections. This love loves you right now, as you are. Yes, even with messy hair, a bad attitude, PMS, a job you hate, and all the other issues that are to be expected in the human realm. Knowing and cultivating Divine Love teaches us how to love ourselves and how to love others *unconditionally*.

I am intimately familiar with not always loving myself. I have even *hated* parts of myself. The part of me that used food for self-soothing? Yeah, I hated her. The part of me that seemed to be more sensitive than everyone else and needed a lot of alone time? Oh, I couldn't stand her. The part of me who didn't have the perfect body, who battled chronic health issues? Ugh, she was my archenemy.

You see, I had done *hundreds* of practices that helped me cultivate my focus and energy (all really great things), but without learning how to *really love* all my messy little selves, those practices only furthered my futile quest for self-perfection. I also got praised for being pretty, sexy, and successful, so I strove for perfection in those realms instead of the only realms that really mattered—self-love and experiencing love for and from the Divine.

And while there is nothing wrong with wanting physical health, beauty, and worldly success, motivating our desires with anything less than love will always leave us thirsting for a fuller completion in our spiritual life. We all crave love, and without it, we turn to other things we hope will give it to us.

This chapter is overflowing with Love Practices. In these practices, the goal isn't self-improvement; it's knowing how to love and be loved. Ironically, the more we walk in that love, the more okay we are with being (perfectly) imperfect.

But Katie, what do you mean by Love?

We could spend a lifetime exploring this question—as many poets, philosophers, and songwriters the world over have! For me, love is what I feel when I connect with the fullness of my unguarded heart. I can feel love flow through me when I am accepting of who I am—and who everyone else is. I feel love when I see all of my messy life as a sacred mandala, that spiritual symbol of inner wholeness.

In terms of connecting to your spiritual life, we can think of love as the feeling that arises naturally within both the body and mind when you feel safe, joyful, seen, appreciated, and fully expressed. It's a heightened state of inner contentment that supersedes temporary circumstances, one in which you feel most connected to the truth of who you are and long to share that with others. Love is knowing your intrinsic goodness and sensing that goodness in the world. Love is expansive. It's inherently attractive. Love is relational, but it's not trying to "fix" you or anyone else. It's generous. It's like a shot of spiritual adrenaline that clears resentment, heals inner wounds, and fuels worthy dreams. Love makes you *glow*.

We often think of love as a feeling of affection toward another person, whether that's a lover, a family member, or a friend. If you've ever had a pet, you've known love. Sometimes a beautiful day—when the temperature is *just so* and the sun and trees and breeze seem to be dancing in concert—can trigger an upswell of love. For a bibliophile, a perfectly crafted sentence might spark a feeling of love. A delicious meal, a child's laugh, a stirring piece of music—love may arise from anything that brings you into a state of giddy, grateful, glowing awareness: In this moment, I wouldn't change a thing. In this moment, what is happening is good. In this moment, something real is here.

And here is a secret: Love is always available.

Another cool thing about love is that it's generative. The more you experience it, the easier it is to experience more of it. It's also inherently creative and uplifting. It sees things and says *yes* to them. Love is all-consuming in that it dissolves resistance and unnecessary suffering. It is empowering in that it gives us energy beyond our individual capacity. And it is intrinsic in that it lives in each of us. Love is holy, because *it has the capacity to hold all things*.

And experiencing love is the fastest and most direct way to connect with the Divine.

Why? Because God is Love.

Let me repeat that. God is Love.

It's truly that simple. But here is the other side of the love-coin: *You are also that love.* And love is the secret sauce that activates your glow.

GETTING THE SOUL GLOW

Think of your heart as an untapped reservoir of endless love. You can shine that love into yourself, into the cells of your own body. You can shine that love toward God. And you can shine it toward others.

We are often running around looking for love in all the wrong places. But the greatest experiences of love can't be found in a church or a mosque, or even at your yoga studio, although these places can *inspire* us toward love. There is only one required element for the ecstasy love can offer, no matter if you find yourself in a prison cell or a vaulted cathedral. That element is *your body*, the sacred, breathing temple that no one can take from you. The altar is your own heart. And the best offering you can make to that love altar is the content of your thoughts and the unfolding experience of your raw emotions.

Love lights this temple and fuels the intention of the altar. Love is the ultimate universal religion.

And through this *embodied* religion, everything we see, touch, taste, hear, and feel becomes holy.

This chapter will help you connect to the love that you already contain through something I call Love Practices. In this light, a spiritual journey is just the process of coming home to love.

A GLOW-WORTHY CONTEMPLATION
The Last Time You Were in Love

When was the last time you felt genuine love? Write about
it. Where were you, and who were you with? What were the
sensations in your body? How did you know it was love?

WHAT DOES LOVE MEAN FOR *YOU*?

"Love is giving somebody happiness."
—My nephew Jack Silcox, age five

Many hold love as a feeling of loving-kindness or compassion. Others see it as passion, mystery, or healthy eroticism. Some see love as the ultimate expression of beauty. Others experience it through gratitude or joy. Still others sense it more as contentment and equanimity. You may feel love in one or more of these expressions, or maybe in another way altogether.

Bottom line: Love is a deeply personal experience, and one that you can tailor to your spiritual life. Whatever else it is for you, love is an energy that raises your spiritual vibration.

✴ A GLOW-WORTHY CONTEMPLATION ✴

Invoking Love in the Body

What words do you use to describe the feeling or energetic state of Love? What words bring you to that vibration?

Try invoking the following loving expressions in your body: kindness, warmth, sweetness, non-judgment, acceptance, compassion, empathy. Whisper the words to yourself and notice what starts to happen inside.

Where does love live in your body? What does it do to your body?

One of my favorite frames for love comes from the Middle Eastern Bahá'í faith. It distinguishes four types of love: love that flows from the Divine to humans, love that flows from humans to the Divine, self-love, and the love we give to and receive from one another.

For practical purposes, we can think of this as a linear process: I feel the love of the Divine for me, and I give it back through gratitude. This is an *active* celebration of the love I feel. As I celebrate love for the Divine and feel it inside myself, it's easier to feel love *for* myself, and in turn, to offer that love easily to others, like a cup that runneth over. We often get it backwards. We look for love from the outside world *first*, thinking it will help us love ourselves and feel worthy of God's love! I mean, how many of us longed for that *one* potential partner, got into a relationship with them, and then still did not fully love ourselves? We are so often looking for our glow in all the wrong places.

In Buddhism, love is defined by a capacity to experience and share freedom. Freedom is the measure, the guide, and the goal of love. In his book *How to Love*, Thich Nhat Hanh equates love to the willingness to deeply understand ourselves and others. He writes, "When our hearts are small, our understanding and compassion are limited, and we suffer . . . but when our hearts expand, these same things don't make us suffer anymore. We have a lot of understanding and compassion and can embrace others."

Shintoism is grounded in a deep love and respect for the sacredness of nature, which allows us to understand nature as its own constant love-resource. Taoism emphasizes the importance of cultivating a feeling of nurturing toward oneself, teaching that love is what flows through all of creation and connects all things.

In *Works of Love*, the Christian philosopher Søren Kierkegaard writes that love is a requirement for following the teachings of Christ. The Bible speaks of four types of love: *eros* (passionate/erotic love), *storge* (familial love), *phileo* (brotherly love, or the love for all of humanity and nature), and *agape* (the highest form: unconditional love).

In the Sufi tradition, *ishq*, or ecstatic love, is the ultimate requirement for accessing the Divine. Love must overtake the practitioner, lifting her into a state of ecstasy where she can merge with the Divine.

While a passionate love affair can act as a *spark* for love, what many of these traditions reveal is that through passionate, even ecstatic love of the Divine, we create a love refuge *for* ourselves, *within* ourselves, and *by* ourselves. This is the opposite of the rigorous asceticism and meticulous ritual observance found in many iterations of traditional religion. Wild, ecstatic love is considered taboo, something *unholy*.

Yet I have found that *without the humbling effect of love*, practices that would otherwise make us more powerful and awake can inflate the ego, burn us out, or turn us brittle. Our world is littered with examples of this: the politico who starts off wanting to help change the world, only to become obsessed with his personal platform; the Christian pastor who focuses more on building up his congregation than building up his own relationship to Christ; or the popular yoga teacher who becomes more interested in growing her brand than growing her inner light. Growing in true power, not ego power, is something we all have to stay vigilant about in our lives.

Without love, intellectual knowledge and scholarly philosophy—no matter how sublime and complex—are devoid of dynamic energy. Love is the red-hot life force of the mind. Without it we are incomplete in our true soul-power.

Love Practice is the blood that nourishes the heart of our broader spiritual practice. Love melts anger, resentment, and fear and brings us into deeper communion with our core essence. Love brings joy. It makes us feel truly full.

Like any discipline, love also requires development and practice. In ancient times, Sufism, Hinduism, Gnosticism, and Judaism all had methods to train the "Student as Lover." And yet today, love is a realm that we so often leave to chance.

The techniques offered here, and throughout this whole book, aim to get you "in the room with love," as one of my Ayurveda mentors, Dr. Claudia Welch, says. Because the truth is, we're not always in that room.

One of my early Ayurveda teachers told me that her mentor would advise her to fall in love *before* she meditated. It was good advice. Without love, all the techniques in the world will still leave us longing for something . . . deeper. And all meditative/prayer-based/spiritual methods are really just laying fertile soil for the seed of an inner love affair to take root.

LIP SERVICE TO LOVE

"Only those who have love will attain God."
—Guru Gobind Singh Ji

We may intuitively sense that love is important for spiritual advancement. Most of us learn the basic moral values of love and kindness as children, whether in school, through a spiritual community, or from our parents. Love is a human universal.

But cultivating love, or even knowing what love is, can be *really* hard. This may ring especially true if you're currently dealing with the many messy emotions that arise from this complicated thing we call life. Let's face it: It's easy to feel loving and peaceful after a yoga practice or a church service. But then when you watch the news or get in an argument with a family member, all those feel-good vibes can fly right out the window.

Love Practices are the way we grow our love muscle so that the normal upsets don't bump us from our spiritual path so easily. The stronger this muscle is, the easier it will be to connect to and stay at your highest spiritual vibration. In this way, your body becomes a living magnet and glowing transmitter of the force of love.

The purpose behind so many spiritual practices—yoga poses, incense, prayers, breath work, meditation, songs, chants, sermons, contemplations—is to prepare the body and mind for presence and love to flow. They refocus your attention on positive, uplifting energy and away from normal mind-chatter or a negative worldview.

Love belongs to no particular group or religion. In fact, many religious traditions and groups hold love as a guiding ethos. But that doesn't mean that they're always going to get it right, either—it's hard to embody love all the time! We've all heard of the peace-and-love hippie commune that gradually turns into a cult, or the church founded on principles of biblical love that becomes just another gossipy social scene.

Our nature as humans makes it easy for us to move into reactivity, fear, and conflict. In fact, our brains are wired to be constantly vigilant for danger. Love Practices help us lay down new neural pathways connecting us to our higher capacities of reason, compassion, belonging, and, yep, love. Research suggests that the oxytocin and dopamine released when we experience love help us open the neural pathways responsible for processing our daily lives, boosting our motivation, and forming emotional bonds. The more we love, the easier it gets. And so, like anything we want to get better at, we need to practice.

I have dedicated much of my life to studying traditions that hold love and compassion as their highest goals. The tradition of Bhakti yoga from India offers beautiful and time-tested practices for cultivating love for and from the Divine. But it certainly isn't the only religion to do so. At its core, Christianity is also all about love. Similarly, the core of Zen is emptiness, and within that emptiness is the fullness of love. And even modern science is getting down with this whole love thing, with emergent evidence for how love changes our brains and bodies (we will get into this later). Even many forms of psychotherapy are about learning to love and heal the wounds of a scared and vulnerable inner child.

In this way, Love Practices are inherently nonsectarian and nonreligious. They can be applied toward any God or Goddess, or none at all!

Throughout this book I will refer to this approach as *bhakti* when referencing Hindu practices and teachers, and Love Practices when speaking more generally.

YOUR BODY ON LOVE

There is a physiological justification for why love and other positive emotions have been such a central part of spiritual life throughout millennia and across cultures. Scientific research consistently connects love with greater intuition, empathy, health, and happiness—in short, wholeness. Love makes us feel holy.

For example, the HeartMath Institute has shown that when participants focus on their actual hearts and generate feelings of love, appreciation, gratitude, or joy, they enter into *coherence*, a state of balance where all the aspects of one's being are in sync and aligned with each other. The institute has found that our hearts' rhythms actually generate electromagnetic fields around our bodies that look like a geometric torus. Unconsciously, these fields are read and interpreted by the nervous systems of others. We can, without words, sense one another's hearts.

Moreover, intensive research done by John and Beatrice Lacey and other scientists shows that our mind and heart are in constant two-way communication. This connection between brain and heart plays a massive role in determining how we perceive the world, how we process our feelings, and whether we can access our deepest intuitive knowledge.

Feelings of love also make us happier, which is proven to have a range of health benefits including better sleep, stronger immunity, and better capacity to deal with chronic pain. This could be due to the release of neurochemicals like oxytocin, which boosts our capacity for bonding, trust, and relationships in general.

Scientific studies have found that practicing seven weeks of meditation on loving feelings dramatically improved positive emotions, a feeling of life purpose, and reduced symptoms of depression and other illnesses. And a 2013 study found that when we meditate on love, we can improve the tone of our vagal nerve, one of the key components of physical health. Other studies reveal the incredible benefits of love- and kindness-based meditations on reducing migraines, PTSD, chronic pain, and negative self-talk.

Beyond these benefits, love has the ability to actually change the way our brain behaves. Researchers have found that the part of our brain responsible for learning new information and changing habits—which becomes less active as we age—becomes *more* active when we're in love. It also activates when we feel a sense of love for something bigger than ourselves—devotion and surrender to a higher power have more in common with interpersonal love than you might think!

Research has also suggested that regularly working with positive, love-based meditations—for as little as ten minutes a day!—helps boost our capacity to emotionally process, feel empathy, connect socially, and handle stress, and can even reduce biological markers for aging.

BHAKTI: THE ULTIMATE PATH OF GLOW

"Oh holy Great flame, grant me with love. You said the
spreading love is Para Brahma (the Highest Form of God),
for the thing which is everywhere is only Love, and Love
is the only thing which is like a soul within us."
—*"Kandha Guru Kavasam"*

As science has found time and time again, meditating on love changes our body's chemistry. But the ancient mystics already knew this. The tradition of bhakti from India is one part of this long history of love practices.

Bhakti is the Sanskrit word for love. It also means devotion or surrender. Another of my favorite definitions of bhakti is "to move toward with affection." Similarly to Tantra, bhakti is both a uniquely Indian religious approach—replete with deeply held traditions, gods, goddesses, rites, and rituals—and a fundamentally human, universal approach to using the emotion of love as a gateway into freedom from our small, limited sense of self. For the purposes of this book, we will approach bhakti in the more universal sense of letting love be our spiritual North Star, rather than in a religious or academic sense.

So far we've been discussing purely presence forms of meditation. Bhakti is slightly different in that it invokes what is known as *rasa dhatu*, or the "juices" of the body. What does that mean? Rasa has many meanings, but in this case, it means we humans live in wet, "sap-filled" bodies rich with hormones, blood, sex fluids, and neurochemicals. And through our thoughts and emotions, we can change the chemistry of those bodily waters to deeply affect our mood.

Bhakti deeply honors the *emotional* reality of being human and guides us to use our emotions, particularly love and affection, to connect to something bigger than ourselves. In other words, we use mood and feeling to connect to Divinity.

Bhakti addresses the broad nature of love, and, like Christianity, undertakes a taxonomy of it. Love can take many forms: sensual, silent, sweet, joyful, expansive, freedom-bringing, subtle, or overt. According to the seminal text the *Narada Bhakti Sutras*, love answers a deep yearning we all carry. All of our desires and longings lead us, at some point, to the deeper desire under the desire: a longing to touch that which is pure, eternal, and unchanging in ourselves and others.

Our relationships, particularly the ones about which our feelings are most intense (either positive or negative), bring us into this experience. We are all operating from both our adaptations (or core wounds)—behaviors we used to survive in the past, but which may no longer be useful (and may now be harming us and others)—and our core nature. The path of bhakti guides us to operate more from the core nature of our souls than from our often-harmful adaptations.

Bhakti also invites Divinity into everyday life through the art of *profound worship*. This means giving focused time and attention to rituals that ignite an inner love-force and soften our hearts. We know bhakti is starting to work when we begin to see ourselves and others, more and more, through the eyes of love.

Another way to connect to love in bhakti is to surrender to the *Ishta Devata*—a phrase meaning a personalized and often personified Divinity. This path isn't for everyone, but if it is your cup of tea, it's really handy. Why? Because it is super helpful for our human mind to anthropomorphize when connecting to the Divine. Bhakti offers us the ultimate smorgasbord of choices when it comes to having a personal life with God: We can approach divinity as a father, mother, friend, or lover, or as a natural force like the sun, moon, or Earth. Anything goes in bhakti, as long as the connection feels real.

We can also use bhakti to hold space around the powerful energies of anger, jealousy, hatred, pride, arrogance, and sadness. And over time, this and other Love Practices have the power to infuse our lives with a sense of what I call mellow joy. Though we might also experience the highs of Divine ecstasy and bliss, long-term spiritual awakening may feel more like standing in a field of steady peacefulness.

LOVE IS YOUR BEST PROTECTION

We may worry that if we are open to love, we will be pushovers or victims. Surrendering to Divinity/Love doesn't make us egoless or passive. It actually makes us extra strong because we become more invincible and resilient when we are motivated by self-love. The great Sufi mystic Rumi described this protective nature of Divine love beautifully: "Love is an emerald. Its brilliant light wards off dragons on this treacherous path."

It's like love has our back!

And while love is protective, it doesn't mean you don't have to stand up for yourself. Actually, it often means doing tough stuff—like loving yourself enough to walk away from things that may harm you or saying no to requests that don't feel in alignment with your needs.

The Hindu goddess Durga is the ultimate symbol of this symbiotic relationship between love and protection. One of the meanings of Durga is "she who is invisible and invincible." (Hint: The invisible/invincible part *is* love.) Another meaning is "impenetrable fortress." But this doesn't mean we should wall ourselves off from the world. Paradoxically, surrendering to love actually makes us *stronger* in love, wiser in love, wilder in love, and more authentically ourselves.

LOVE IS A MUSCLE

Ask any middle-school parent and they will tell you: If their kid doesn't practice the violin, they will suck at the violin and make everyone miserable every time they pick the thing up. Similarly, if you don't practice love, you will most likely suck at love. I feel I can make this bold statement because, after decades of working with people, I have yet to meet anyone who had such enlightened, love-filled, Buddha-parents that they needed no practice in love.

I spent years studying the key texts of bhakti, and one of my favorites is the *Narada Bhakti Sutras*. This text speaks of *Aparabhakti* (Lower Love), which is the training path required to prime our bodies and minds toward love. We all know we want ultimate love, but we need the means and methods. Love is a muscle. And like any muscle, it must be built and trained. The following practices will take us to the love-gym, spiritually preparing us to both give and receive the spontaneous grace of love.

Lower Love might look like rolling out your practice mat and entering into a prayer or meditation. It might mean intentionally doing something nice for yourself or a loved one. It might mean placing a stack of uplifting books by your bed to remind yourself of your commitment to love. It might mean volunteering at your local elder center to remind yourself that all stages of life are sacred. These are all practices that can lead to love.

Then there is *Parabhakti* (Higher Love), which is the union with love itself. When you reach this state, all the methods and techniques of Lower Love melt away and can be let go of because you are already resting in love. Higher Love is effortless and continual love.

In other words, Higher Love is a *state of consciousness* where you exist in a place of love. You see the world through the eyes of love because you have truly and deeply learned that love is who you really are.

THE HOLY PAUSE

Transformative love requires not just feeling, but action and attention. What does this mean? It means that even if you love someone with your whole heart, if you ignore them, your love is not the kind of love that can melt wounds or be transformational in their life. A father can deeply love his son, but if he works all day and never looks him in the eye or listens to him, his love is incomplete.

The same holds true with you. You can kinda love yourself, but if you don't take the time, every day, to check in with yourself to see what has arisen in the course of your life, your love is incomplete. There will be parts of you that feel abandoned. Parts that, like the son in the example above, feel unattended to.

Thich Nhat Hanh puts it this way: "Love is the capacity to take care, to protect, to nourish. If you are not capable of generating that kind of energy toward yourself—if you are not capable of taking care of yourself, of nourishing yourself, of protecting yourself—it is very difficult to take care of another person. Love is a practice."

That is why the most powerful Love Practice on the planet may be what I call the Holy Pause, which is essentially a practice in presence. It takes a few seconds, but those few seconds are often the bravest, scariest, and most radical seconds of your life. It is that intentional gap that gives us time enough that we do not react automatically ("Okay, how can I distract myself from what feels uncomfortable in myself?") but rather become responsive ("Let me pause and deeply attend to what is here or seek support if it is too much.").

Simply stated: *The Holy Pause is a doorway into actual self-love. It is a powerful message to your subconscious that says, "You are worthy of presence. I am here."*

✴ A GLOW-WORTHY MEDITATION ✴
The Holy Pause

The Holy Pause is a simple practice. All you have to do is stop and make the commitment to be with yourself. If you just read this practice rather than experiencing it, it may sound super cheesy. But the thing is, the stressed-out parts of yourself are not complex or mature. They often need simple, direct, and loving communication.

The Holy Pause is a brave act in our nonstop, don't-feel world. It is the remedy for society's emphasis on urgency. It is the culture-busting, lineage-defying radicality of stopping the momentum of your day and taking a moment to feel. It is the only place of true rest for the mind and a balm for the soul.

There is no one right way to do the Holy Pause, but below is a script of what works for me. I find that it helps me to place my hand on my heart. Feel free to say these words out loud or silently to yourself.

Feel the contact of the palm of the hand and its weight on your heart.

Attune to your breath.

Say to yourself, silently or aloud:

"I'm here and I've got you."

"I'll never leave you."

"I can be with you in this."

"I can hold you in this feeling. I can stay with you in this moment."

"I am wise enough to be here, now, with you, in this."

"Whatever I've been running from, I can take a moment to feel."

*As you say these things to yourself, notice if there is a signal in
your body of something loving and organizing. Is there something
silent but stable? Is there something wordless and supportive?*

*Anchor, over and over again, through reminding yourself that you
are here. That there is ease in this Holy Pause and that in this
brave moment an alchemy of transformation is occurring.*

CREATING A GLOWING LIFE OF DAILY LOVE RITUALS

In addition to the Holy Pause, here are some other time-tested (and science-backed) practices to get the love-flow going. Try picking a few to begin incorporating more love energy into your life. You may find that one practice fills you up more than another, and that's totally okay. The point is to find whatever helps you have the experience of loving and being loved.

Love Songs

Have you ever noticed that there are some songs that cause even the most stoic to shed a tear? That is the power of music. It bypasses the intellect and goes straight to the emotional and vibrational body.

In the darkest times, singing songs of love and devotion is one of the most powerful ways to help us return to the light. Truly there is something magical about music and singing as expressions of devotion—which may explain why we see them in spiritual traditions the world over.

Science shows us how singing songs of praise changes our brain. Those songs can be traditional religious chants, hymns, or anything that brings you into a state of feeling more love. Just make sure they're something you *feel*, because it's your *intention and loving focus* that spark the magic. You need to get *real* about what you sing about. You cannot fake it.

As you sing, offer the words and sounds to something bigger than your intellect. As you continue singing, keep offering your thoughts to the sounds themselves. With time and practice, you will be able to discern between thought, feeling, and that sacred realm of the vibrational—a full-bodied sense of resonance that is neither thought nor something solely physical. Use the song to ring yourself like a gong—letting the sound go straight into the core of who you are. The vibrational quality of music is purifying, and the mantras and sounds awaken what sleeps within us.

Not only does music awaken and purify emotion, it also rouses the dormant spiritual qualities within us, lifting us above the everyday and into something ecstatic. Lost and hidden facets of ourselves come alive in music: vulnerability, tenderness, power, joy, and hope are reactivated, and we are reminded of who we really are.

As you sing, think of opening your heart into the sweetness of not having to know, plan, achieve, or do. In bhakti, a sacred contemplation is to become aware of *who* is listening as you chant alone. While singing, the singer begins to notice a wave of love arising. The longer we sing, the more we can feel that love wave merging us into an oceanic love, where the distinction between the self and the Eternal melts away.

How to do it: Identify a song or sacred chant that always moves you. I love any mantra of the Buddhist female deity Tara. I also love old gospel hymns and even a few cheesy love songs. Find your own love songs—the ones that touch your heart—and make a playlist. If you play an instrument, get sheet music. If you don't know the songs by heart, look up the lyrics online. And then, whether it's in your car, at home alone, or out on a walk with your dog, sing your heart out. Yep, *out loud*. And feel it! Don't worry about the quality of your voice (John Legend and Kelly Clarkson aren't judging you). This is about getting *out of your head* and *into your heart*. Repeat as often as possible.

Love Movement

Clearly there is a difference between mindful movement like yoga, sacred dance, and tai chi, and just going to the gym and hitting the treadmill (add to that watching the news in a bad mood and you are in a *really* different realm). But if we exercise with focus and intention, we can bring love into all of our movement practices by exercising with focus and intention. We can make movement *bhaktified* by being present in the body and cultivating good feelings and thoughts as we move. This is called *bhavana,* the intentional cultivation of good vibes.

How to do it: It's easy. *Any physical movement/exercise + intentional good feelings = more love.*

Love Intention and Love Dissolving

You don't need to sing or move to become bhaktified—bhavana is enough. Traditionally, we practice bhavana through smarana and laya. *Smarana* means "to remember." It invites us to invoke a memory of a past experience that reminds us of the emotional state of love we want to feel now. Once we have the memory, we can bring in the sensory experience of it, attempting to recreate the details in our mind of how it felt to be there. For example, all I have to do is think of my niece Clara's little face, and I am filled with loving warmth.

Then, we do the practice of *laya*, which means "to dissolve." Once we have the memory, and our body is all juiced up on it, we let go of the memory and focus on the feeling of love *in our body.* Then we let that feeling of love itself be our object of meditation. Once there, we let ourselves dissolve more and more into love until it becomes our entire sense of self.

Again, this doesn't mean thought and other emotions won't also be present, but we continually attend to love as our object of focus. We also learn to identify ourselves more with the *love* than with those ever-changing thoughts, images, and feelings. This practice is the cornerstone of my personal spiritual walk, and I will guide you through it at the end of this chapter as well as in our recorded meditations.

✳ A GLOW-WORTHY MEDITATION ✳

Remembering Love

Take a moment to find your breath, to feel your heart, and to attune to the realest version of you. The sincere you. The vulnerable you. The you that holds both light and dark. The spark of your personality that those who truly love you see.

*Feel the weight of your body like a gift, pulling you
down into this moment. Here and now.*

Attune to your breath. Notice the rise and fall of the inhale and exhale.

Feel the gentle pause at the top of the inhale and bottom of the exhale.

Follow every millimeter of the breath. As if it mattered. As if it were enough.

*Relax more and more deeply into accepting every
aspect of this moment, inner and outer.*

*Now, move your attention down your body and into the earth, like a
golden chord or a waterfall moving down the back of your body. Breathe
for a few minutes, continuing to move your attention into the earth.*

Let your eyes soften and become even more receptive.

Let your heart soften and become even more receptive.

Let your belly soften and become even more receptive.

Let your legs soften and release into the ground.

*You to you—in all of your beautiful and broken parts, all of your
wanted and unwanted parts. This presence is behind the persona
that you present to the world, as well as the scared little girl inside
of you that is ashamed, angry, and scared and wants to hide.*

*Now, as you feel more settled into your body, remember a
moment in your life when you felt very much in love. Make sure
not to choose a moment that causes pain. Pick a pure moment.
It can involve the love of a child, a pet, a sunset, a moment at
work or volunteering—a time when you really felt of higher
service or a deeply tender moment with a friend or beloved.*

*See the moment very clearly in your mind. Let the sensations,
feelings, textures, and images of that moment come to you. With
the image clear, can you feel the love in your body? Where do
you notice it? Where does it live in your body? Does it make*

you feel warm? Is there a sense of belonging? Do you feel small?
Big? Tingling? Awake? Held? Expanded? Relaxed?

Really feel *the memory of the love in your body.*

Once you have "found the love" in your body, you don't need the
memory. Simply meditate on the love. Let yourself become ever more
interested and curious about the state of love unfolding in you. If you
lose your way and become distracted by thoughts or pulled into other
feelings or states, come back to the memory of love, and then return
to the feeling of the love in the body. Meditate on that feeling.

Love Surrender

One of the central ways we connect to God is by surrendering ourselves *into* love. It's not that we are giving ourselves up. Or that we surrender ourselves because we are some worthless worm who can be redeemed only by dissolving into a higher power. Not at all. We surrender our limited sense of self, our limited perceptions, into *who we truly are.* In this way, we aren't going away, we are becoming more ourselves.

If the idea of this Divine surrender into a Higher Love scares you, take heart. In his book *Yoga: The Greater Tradition,* David Frawley writes that the ultimate expression of bhakti yoga is surrender to the Divine *as one's inner self.* You are surrendering into your own inner love.

The path, he says, consists of concentrating one's mind, emotions, and senses on the Divine Mother, like an inner parent. But here's the kicker: The wisest, kindest part of you *is* the Divine Mother. Or Divine Father. Or Lover. Or Planetary Cosmic Christ Oneness. Or Pagan Nature Witch. Whatever terminology or relationship works for you is wonderful. (For me, some days I need God as a boundary-setting father. Other days a great-grandmother. Other days, an infinite, genderless presence of cosmic love beyond space and time.) In other words, true Divine surrender is nothing more than a surrender to who you actually are.

✳ A GLOW-WORTHY MEDITATION ✳
A Personal Connection to the Holy

There are as many ways to connect to the Divine as there are beings on the planet. The purpose of this meditation is to connect with something authentic—God, Divinity, Presence, the Tao . . . whatever name feels right to you. You can work with a particular god or goddess (Jesus or Kali, for example), or with supports like sacred images, symbols, nature, divine parents, benign spirits, supportive ancestors, angels, or even just the sense that You Are Not Alone In The World.

This meditation may be slightly different each time you approach it. Stay curious. Let the images and sensations inform you.

Take a moment to allow yourself that Holy Pause. Attune to your breath if that helps. Begin to let your awareness drop in and down inside your body, all the way from the top of your head to the tips of your toes and into the earth. Spend some time grounding yourself in the fabric of your physicality. It's natural to notice thoughts and ruminations, but keep tuning in to the sensations of the body and channeling your attention in and down.

Now, once you feel a little calmer, hold the intention of inviting in something bigger than yourself, something bigger than your normal thinking mind. Invite in spiritual support. The feeling of being receptive, quiet, and invitational is paramount. To be blunt, get your intellect out of the way.

It may be a version of God you already feel connected to, or it may be simply an openness to receiving spiritual guidance. For me, I will often get the sense that I am no longer alone, that there is something holding me, embracing me, surrounding me, or sitting with me. Other times, I will get an image of a sacred teacher, friend, or symbol. The practice becomes magical when we are open to receiving sacred support and don't have a preconceived idea of what or who may show up. Once you feel that sacred support has arrived,

feel your embodied self and that sacred support in relationship to one another.
Invite it to come closer, to come into your worries, fears, sadness, and personal
issues. Continue to rest in that relationship between you and the Holy.

Love Service

Simply stated, Love Service is doing positive, uplifting things for others without the expectation of any return. These everyday actions are offerings you are making to Divinity. And it's even more powerful when you do these nice things and no one knows about it but you.

Once, I was in an Uber with a friend. We were asking the driver some friendly questions, and it came out that his wife, only thirty-five, was very sick with lupus. With three kids, a full-time day job, and an ailing spouse, he was forced to drive an Uber at night to keep up with the bills. As we departed the cab, I saw my friend hand him a twenty-dollar bill. Afterwards, I kept thinking about his story, and that night I tipped him again on the app, just wanting to send some small token of support his way.

It's important to understand that Love Service has nothing to do with being *seen* as generous. It is simply the response to a need. Today I can help you, knowing that tomorrow it may be me who is in need. Sometimes, in our disconnected world, we must actively seek out opportunities to be of service. Find ways of doing acts of service with no expectation of recognition. That's the point!

How to do it: Take a moment to enter into the Holy Pause. When you feel quiet, ask yourself the question: *Who or what can I serve today that has nothing to do with my own ego's aggrandizement?*

Let the answer come.

It may be volunteering at your local soup kitchen or Big Sister organization. It may be making some food for that friend whose mom is in the hospital. Perhaps it's a simple financial donation to a worthy cause. Sometimes you may even hear, *In order for you to be of best service to your family, you need to book a massage and chill the heck out.* In other words, sometimes the best way we can serve other people is by making sure we have our own inner tank of energy full enough to be of actual help.

Love Altars

Think of an altar as an external location to place your inner feeling and a sacred reminder of holiness. It acts as a visual, tangible representation of—and reminder to cultivate—love, compassion, or any spiritual intention. It is a place where we remember the sacred, eternal quality of life. We make altars to remind us of the things that are most important to us—like the evolution of our spirit, our loved ones, and our connection to symbols, gods, goddesses, and nature. (We will go into altars more deeply in the Ritual chapter.)

How to do it: Creating an at-home altar might involve setting up a special table or shelf with an image or representation of your connection to the Divine. Traditionally, altars include scent (often in the form of oils), flowers, incense, candles, and water. They may also hold photos of mentors, teachers, or relatives. My altar includes a hodgepodge of deities from across the religious spectrum, pictures of my family and mentors, and seasonal objects.

Love Prayers

So many of us have lost prayer practices from our childhood, or have no experience with prayer at all. For some of us, the thought of praying makes our stomachs turn. Think of prayers as sacred petitions we present to the Divine. They can be acts of praise and worship, devotion, or confession. Meditation teacher and author Tara Brach says that one of the simplest prayers is just saying the word "Help." Whereas meditation is getting quiet enough to hear and listen to God's voice, prayer is talking to God directly. It may be helpful to think of prayer as having a real conversation with Divinity—while also having a conversation with the highest aspect of our own being.

How to do it: Pray in your own words and in your own voice. Be real. Pour your heart out to the Divine and trust that you are being heard. Journal your prayer if that feels more comfortable than speaking, whether aloud or silently. Read the prayers of others and tap into what resonates for you.

My inner prayers are usually a variation on this:

Dear God,
Please come and be with me.
I feel like a hot mess.
I have forgotten who I really am.
I feel lost and alone. Scared. Angry. Confused.
I have forgotten my worth and lovability.
I feel like a little girl again.
Please come and be with me. And help me be with myself.
Show me who I am beyond this body and mind.
Help me loosen the binds on my mind that keep me in limiting thoughts
and negativity.
Help me open my heart where it feels constricted.
Help me receive the grace and love that I know is all around me.
Please be with me now in this.
I am open and receptive.
I will try to be patient.
And hold faith that, no matter what . . .
I can remember that, when I call you, Spirit, you will come.

WHEN IT'S NOT ALL LOVE AND LIGHT

When we're cultivating love, we need to be careful about *spiritual bypassing*—skipping over the parts of our experience that don't feel positive or socially acceptable. When we do this, we are refusing to tend to the truth. We send all of our bad or uncomfortable feelings out of the realm of our consciousness, pretending we are all "cupcakes and bubble baths," when what we actually may be is pissed off. Think Dolores Umbridge from the Harry Potter movies. The pink cardigan–wearing teacher who is all smiles on the surface is secretly a despotic monster who hates children. She is the hilarious embodiment of spiritual bypassing.

Modern self-help culture has fostered a false and dangerous idea that being committed to love is antithetical to being open and willing to experience all of our authentic human emotions, including the so-called negative ones. But that's not what love is about at all. For our journey, think of love as your spiritual immune system. You can also think of it as the container, something in and around you where you can work with all of the gnarly stuff that you experience in this life. Love is the matrix within which any *true* transformation takes place, whether that transformation is a social change movement, healing in your body, or working with tough memories and emotions from your past.

Moreover, as you begin to deepen your spiritual life, it is often the case that you will feel *more*, not less. As you bring in more love and light, it's like pouring water into a dry ink well. What does the water dredge out first? All of that old, crusty ink. Then, it's our job to digest those resurfaced feelings and not reactively blow them out on everyone else.

Often when I sit to meditate, I feel way worse than when I'm running around distracting myself. It's as if everything that had been sitting in my mind and in my heart, everything I've been avoiding feeling, bubbles to the surface. In that moment, it sucks, but if I can bring in a loving presence, that presence begins to dissolve those uncomfortable emotions. In this way, love softens and dissolves the discomfort from my predictable reactions and thoughts. Over time, these so-called negative emotions begin to become more and more familiar to us. In fact, they may never fully leave us. We just get better at recognizing that they *aren't* us.

LASTLY . . .

Love Practice is intense. On the surface love may seem like a flowery, Pollyanna, lighthearted thing. It is not. It is a path for only the bravest. In fact, the ancient bhakti yoga teachings say that love is the greatest of all yogic paths. All paths end in the *fire* of love. (They said fire!)

This whole book is a practice manual for learning to love yourself and others in a more authentic way. As we move on, keep coming back to the principles of love you learned here. Let love be the foundation that upholds every single thing you read and practice as we go forward. When you lose your way, come back to the starting point—that you are loved in this moment, no matter how yucky life may feel.

Love Practice is an ongoing journey. I myself am a half-baked love-muffin still working it out in the oven. Every day, I stumble. As you commit to Love Practice, please expect to constantly start over. And remember: Stumbling toward love is an intrinsic part of remembering your glow.

6

Energy

I f love is the matrix, *prana* is the electricity that brings that matrix to life. It's the power that flows through love's veins and makes it active in the world.

Prana is energy. It is everywhere. Always. And in limitless supply, even when we don't feel it. To access a sense of prana, we have to learn to attune to the subtle. We do this by refining our focused attention, opening our heart, and learning some basic rules.

Working with energy, like love, takes practice. We are building a new muscle. It also takes focus, precisely because most of us were trained to mainly be conscious of the physical body, outer distractions, and our endlessly thinking mind. Most of us did not receive an education in the subtler aspects of who we are.

But there is good news: We hold an unaccessed reservoir of power, whether we are aware of it or not.

This forgetfulness around our energy doesn't make it any less real. It's like the classic metaphor of a fish who doesn't understand the concept of water despite swimming in it constantly: We don't observe the energy all around us because we haven't been taught that it exists. We are fish swimming in an energy ocean. And once you start working with energy, it feels so good, you may become a prana lover, too.

Working with energy is your human birthright. Energy is one of the primary tools of healing in all ancient traditions, across all continents, and the benefits of working with energy are life-changing. Prana doesn't care about the color of your skin, your gender, or your belief systems. Prana is truly the thing that unites not only all humans, but all of life on Earth. And it is as alive in you today as it was in the yogi, the medicine woman, and the reiki healer from time immemorial.

WHAT IS PRANA?

Prana is life's electrical current. I think of it as a swirling, intelligent, electric love. Like a spiderweb, it weaves itself through all things and links all of us together as a global community. It is endlessly flowing everywhere. When we are awake to our prana, we can use it to take us where we want to go. If we are not awake to prana, it will lead us down our usual energy tendencies, and those of our family lineage (more on that later).

Prana is the basis of much of the Hindu, Ayurvedic, hatha yoga, and Tantric yoga traditions. Also known as *vayu*, or the wind god, prana is often associated with breath. It is said to flow through the nervous system by way of 72,000 *nadis*, or energy channels, but its primary homes are the brain, heart, and belly. These are the core energy points that circulate prana throughout the entire body.

The understanding of prana transcends the continent of India. Most indigenous and spiritual traditions have given this force their own names. In the Christian tradition, we call it *Sophia*. Traditional Japanese medicine refers to it as *ki*, and Chinese medicine as *chi*. It is known as *baraka* in the Islamic tradition and *ruah* in Judaism. The Māori culture calls it *mana*. The ancient Greeks called it *pneuma*. Buddhist monk Thich Nhat Hanh calls it the "energy of mindfulness." In the West, scientists at the HeartMath Institute have studied it through the electrical pulses our hearts and brains emit. The hippies in the US in the 1960s called it "good vibrations."

Western culture strongly encourages us to identify with the physical body only on the most superficial of levels. We've been conditioned to strive to make it attractive and healthy. And while it's a great idea to care deeply for the health of the body and keep it strong and vital, the body is also something we are all going to eventually lose. And that is scary. Most of us spend a lot of time trying *not* to think about death, while simultaneously obsessing about our outer body. Our society helps us avoid the fear of death—or even the thought of death—by selling us the latest fitness trend, superfood, or longevity aid.

Many of us are also very aware of our mental selves, especially when our minds won't stop racing, or we find ourselves falling into negative thought patterns. It's really not our fault. Modern culture emphasizes mental intelligence and verbal capacity. We are trained from childhood to measure our value by how well we perform intellectually (think report cards). And while it's great to get a scholarship to college for sports or mental prowess, no one is offering up scholarships to the best teen energy-worker in town.

Lucky for us, the ancients understood that we are much more than a physical and mental being. We are also an energy being! We have a *prana body*! And by the end of this book, your prana bod is gonna be gorgeous.

Prana comes from the Sanskrit root *pra*, which means "existing first or before," and *ana, an,* or *aniti,* meaning "to breathe." Imagine that—the ancient yogis were able to see an energy that *precedes* the breath of life. The word *prana* suggests that there is something behind the material, animating it and moving it around. This activating force behind matter gives life to all things. Imagine it as the vibrations between the atoms, molecules, and cells of your body. Imagine it as God's light socket. What use is a lamp (your body) if you don't plug it in? That's prana. And we all have this inner light.

Prana is also the power behind our breath, thoughts, nervous system, and emotions. While our physical body handles the mechanics of life, prana is the remarkable force that keeps our blood pumping, our heart beating, and our metabolic processes functioning optimally. Western medicine might relate to prana as the impulses behind the nervous system. It is the aspect of our body's intelligence that we don't have to consciously manage.

For example, you don't have to plan breathing; it just happens. There is something that moves your diaphragm for breath without your having to tell it to do so. That "something" is the energy that rides along all the autonomic and spontaneous processes of life that go unnoticed. The intelligence that beats your heart and pumps your blood without your trying. The intelligence that maintains all the different biochemical waters in the body at a homeostatic level.

Ayurveda classifies prana more broadly, across many of our biological systems, seeing its primary quality as being dynamic, communicative, mobile, and expansive. The reason that we feel better after a yoga or spin class is because we have changed our prana. We have moved energy that may have been stuck in our shoulders from a long day of working at a computer, along with other minor blockages that may have built up.

Energy and thought have a correlative relationship. Energy gets stuck in old patterns when we think the same yucky thoughts, day in and day out. "Oh, I will never be able to leave this job." "I will never find love." "My body (finances, partner, life, etc.) will never change."

Unlike our readily apparent physical and mental selves, prana is more subtle and often requires a deeper connection to inner stillness and mental ease to feel and work with. Connecting with our prana takes us into our ethereal body, and through that subtle work we access deeper (and progressively more hidden) layers of who we are. Prana exists in between the purely material, dense world (think rocks) and the ethereal world (think angels). It is neither purely physical nor purely nonphysical.

The Tantric tradition says that your body is like an island floating in an endless sea of prana. Imagine that for a moment. And the only reason we don't experience that ocean of energy is that we are moving our energy in habitual, more constricted patterns. Usually this involves what is wrong in our lives and how hard or impossible it will be to overcome those things. This is a sign that our prana is contracted.

Tantric tradition also emphasizes that this force, like a Divine Mother, is always available. We just have to ask. I remember my yoga teacher Mohan telling me that "God is waiting on you to take the first step. And after you do, he will take a thousand steps to you, running." This is the power of prana.

PRANA AS GUIDING INTELLIGENCE

There is something universal about prana that we instinctively gravitate toward irrespective of background. Why? Because this energy isn't just animating our bodies, *this energy is the companion of our spirit,* allowing us to give and receive spiritual love. The yogis saw it as the gateway between the body and the soul, as well as between the individual and the Divine. Not only that, but prana enables us to find our true self in this lifetime, and to allow that self to *fully express itself.*

We all want to be around authentically soulful people who seem to glow. We see this in our language: "She has great energy." "He gives off bad vibes." "That woman really lights up a room." We sense something emanating from people like this even before they speak.

Places also hold high- or low-vibe prana. Prana is the reason the Neolithic Britons built Stonehenge, and why today we want to travel to Machu Picchu: We can feel the grandeur of the energy there. It's why the ancient Indians held the Himalayas to be the sacred grounds for enlightenment. There are many places on Earth where we can just *feel* why ancient traditions held them as sacred sites.

There are no rules around places and energy—while certain sites may hold an energy of their own, the energy you feel in a place can also be personal and dependent on you and your history with it. I have nothing against places like Target and IKEA, with their endless mazes of stuff, but, as my family will tell you, "Katie can only last about fifteen minutes in a Walmart." I just start to feel kinda "off." On the contrary, lay me down in the grass beside my house and I can stay there for hours. Give me a forest or a beautiful Roman cathedral and I'm a happy energy-camper. I can sense when a place is sacred—whether it's a river bank, a swimming hole, or a temple. And I can feel when a place has dead or stagnant energy.

✲✱ A GLOW-WORTHY CONTEMPLATION ✲✱
Tuning in to the Subtle

What people in your life light you up?

What places hold a sacred energy for you? Why?
Do they fill you up? Make you feel calm?

What places and people drain you? How do you notice this?

Prana is more than just feeling good vibes in people and places. It is an evolutionary force. It is what brings things into action. It is what causes change, whether in the physical world or the spiritual. Prana is also how we connect to everything—self, friends, lovers, animals, nature, and God. Prana is a big part of our immune system—especially given that much of immunity is about cellular communication, and is affected by the extent to which we feel connected to our outer world.

Prana is the life force that exists between things. It is what exists within the space between me and you. And some traditions say it is a loving thing, this prana. That's good news!

But prana is not only loving—it is also smart. Not like me-and-you smart. Like otherworldly, miraculous smart. Think of prana as an acorn. Hold that acorn in your mind's eye. Now imagine a massive oak tree. That tree is what you are capable of becoming. Everything, all of the information needed to become that big oak, is held in that tiny acorn.

✲✱ A GLOW-WORTHY CONTEMPLATION ✲✱
Your Energetic Landscape

As you contemplate your own prana, it may be helpful to answer these questions:

*How much do you feel like you're on the cutting edge
of your life, living your holy purpose?*

How adaptable are you?

*When you wake up in the morning, how excited do you
feel about the life you get to live? How inspired?*

How expressive do you feel? Creative? Expansive? Enthusiastic about life?

How connected do you feel to yourself? To God? To your world?

*How grounded do you feel? Do you have a deep
sense of being in your feet, legs, and belly? Or
do you live in your heart and/or head?*

Does it feel like your body is alive? Glowing?

Are you in love with your life, even with its ups and downs?

WHAT ABOUT PRANAYAMA?

Many cultures use the conscious control of the breath to alter energy; in India the traditional breathwork practice is known as *pranayama*. There are many great books and resources on the topic, but we will not be going in that direction in this book. Why? Because much influence has been placed on *controlling* prana. Think of it like this: There is a masculine way of working with prana that is focused and controlled, and a feminine way of working with prana that is receptive and soft. We'll focus instead on becoming sensitive to energy and loosely guiding it, rather than more forceful methods of breathwork.

There is nothing wrong with channeling and guiding energy. That's the way things get created—think buildings and roadways, or even cooking a meal. We need to harness and channel energy just to be alive. But when we focus *only* on control, without also cultivating our ability to attune ourselves to the energy itself, we will not hold a *reverence* for this force.

The approach to energy/breathwork in this section will be very gentle. If you want more on breathwork methods as well as an overview of their benefits, please refer to the resource section in the back of this book.

TIME OF DAY AND YOUR ENERGY

If there is one thing we can say about energy, it's that it changes. While always present, energy is also always moving. Throughout a 24-hour day, energy changes cyclically. Think of the times of day as having their own personalities. These changes affect us deeply on an energetic level, even if we don't notice. For example, I used to think I was the only one who felt tired after lunch, and at times even a little more emotional and negative in the afternoon. Then I started studying Ayurveda, which explained that our ancestors have been getting the afternoon blahs for thousands of years. Now that I know what's going on, I can take it less personally.

In Ayurveda, the morning (from around 6 to 10 a.m.) is considered the most energetically sluggish time of day, as we arise out of the heaviness of slumber. It's a good time to get energy *moving* by doing things like breathwork, exercise, and self-care practices. During the midday period (from around noon to 2 p.m.), we have the most fiery and intense energy. It's a great time to ride the energy to get stuff done and engage with the world, while also being careful not to burn out.

The afternoon (from around 2 to 6 p.m.) is when our energy is the most erratic. During this time of day, we are most likely to encounter our undigested thoughts and emotions. We may also recognize our exhaustion at this time, since our physical energy is low while our mental energy is high. I personally start to notice more anxiety, loneliness, or sadness at this time. Others may experience afternoon blues.

Some of us (including me, every now and then!) *resist* these feelings and the natural downswing in energy and go for the 3 p.m. Starbucks double espresso—or my favorite, green tea and dark chocolate. But if possible, we should use the afternoon for a little rest or restorative yoga (hello, Spanish siesta?). It's also a great time for reflection and meditation, as well as creative mental pursuits like art, poetry, reading, or writing.

I know it isn't possible for everyone to take a siesta or write poetry from 2 to 6 p.m. every day, but just knowing that the energy of that time is erratic and ungrounded will help you balance it. Do what you can to pause *for even a few minutes* during your work day. Breathe your awareness through your belly and legs into the ground. Do some of the audio practices I offer at the end of this chapter. And remember, one of the best things about working with energy is that you can do it at work, on a date, in a meeting . . . and no one knows you are doing it!

WORKING WITH ENERGY

Our body's energy is one of the most powerful gateways into connection to the Divinity, and we can even understand the word *Goddess* as a synonym for prana. Many traditions see prana as the gateway to the soul, or truest self. Working with our energy enables us to have a reference point for who we are that is deeply internal rather than dependent on the outside world. Working with prana is a practical path to self-love and self-esteem. Rather than just writing an affirmation and repeating it, prana helps us recognize and experience our true worth.

In our prana practice, we work to hold and circulate more prana inside, rather than constantly pouring it out. For many of us, our typical unconscious tendency is to move energy up and out. When we think, talk, drive, and work on the computer, energy is leaving our body. When we help our kids, energy moves out. When we fight with our partners, energy moves out. Energy master Rosalyn Bruyere, who has the rare gift of seeing energy, says that most Westerners are walking around with all of their energy from the heart up. When they interact, they pour it up and outward. Most of us are in dire need of moving our energy down, not up.

Even more disturbing is that this lack of grounded energy (think belly to legs to earth) actually *keeps us from feeling our own feelings,* as the upper realms of the body are where we interact with the energies of others and feel *their* feelings. If you can't channel energy through your legs, you may not know what you are feeling at all, and thus may experience the feelings of others as your own! Not. Great.

Moreover, energy needs to be able to move down in order for us to rest, relax, and sleep. No wonder we all feel exhausted but can't fall asleep.

HOW DO WE GET OUR ENERGY GROUNDED AND KEEP IT INSIDE?

We keep our energy grounded and inside our bodies by guiding our attention and letting the divine internal power circulate. This involves cultivating a deep sense of both intention and surrender, noticing the subtle internal sensations, images, and impulses of the wild city that is our human body. As we pay attention, a new, intuitive intelligence begins to guide us, reveal insights, and heal us. This doesn't necessarily mean that working with prana will help you cure every disease and resolve every emotional issue. But what it does mean is that you will learn to recenter yourself in the original source of where all life comes from, a river of energy inside of you. It means you get to go home.

I'm an expert on this precisely because getting grounded and feeling embodied has been so difficult for me. I am not a naturally grounded person and I can easily get overwhelmed by my own experience. But now, when I'm with others, I have learned to pay attention to being in myself, rather than merged into them. And over the years, out of sheer necessity, I have greatly ameliorated so many issues (anxiety, "taking on" other people's feelings, dissociation, insomnia . . .) through the very practices I am sharing with you in this chapter and this book.

TEN BASIC PRECEPTS FOR WORKING WITH ENERGY

I have worked with many energy masters around the world and have read a stack of energy-focused books from floor to ceiling. The following precepts for working with energy distill the practices that have rung true in my own experience, with the life force inside me. Keep these in mind when we get to the meditation on energy at the end of this chapter.

1. Thought follows energy and energy follows thought. Change your thoughts and the way you feel will change. Change your energy and the way you think will change.

2. Energy follows focus (aka where you direct your attention).

3. Every energy that exists in the outside world exists within you.

4. We exist in an endless sea of healing energy. Within that sea is also a lot of darkness, but the sea itself is endlessly benevolent. We can't access it unless we fully invite it in with total faith.

5. Energy can't flow as freely through fear, tension, hate, resentment, doubt, unforgivingness, and guilt.

6. Energy loves a good image. Sometimes our brain needs to imagine energy as swirling light, golden honey, hot lava, a blue river, moonlight, and so on. Use whatever visual feels right in the moment.

7. Energy is not seen (usually). Energy is not thought about. Energy is *felt* (which makes writing about it kinda tricky . . .). It's like trying to write about the color blue. Sometimes it's easier to know what prana is by knowing what it is *not*. If you are thinking/judging/planning/talking shit about yourself, you have left the realm of prana.

8. We must learn to both give and receive energy. Most of us are better at one of these things than the other. In my experience, many women are better at giving it out than allowing it to fill them up.

9. Energy can dissolve and resolve blocks, obstructions, and past pain.

10. When working with energy, stay soft, yet resolved. Don't take this all too seriously. All my energy-worker teachers have been very funny. And the best ones have been very humble as well.

THE DANCE OF GIVING AND RECEIVING

So much of how we feel in our day-to-day life is determined by the quality, quantity, and directionality of our energy. Our prana landscape directly affects our immune system. It also determines our ability to be creative, make decisions, and feel happy. Our capacity to draw in positive energy from our environment is directly related to our level of stress. When we are tense, we become contracted, and our life force cannot freely flow. To be healthy, we need to be able to both give energy and let it release. We need to be able to take in positive energy with our five senses, through things like loving touch, high-vibe food, and the natural world around us. We also need to be able to give—in the form of service, generosity, and attention, but also by cultivating a sense of non-attachment toward the objects and mindsets we cling to.

One of the boons of working with energy is that it can reveal your tendencies: Are you better at giving or receiving? Is it easier for you to float above your head or do you get stuck in the heavy ground? Is all of your attention out in front of you? Or are you pulled back? As you practice the energy work at the end of the chapter, notice these tendencies and begin to cultivate their opposite within you. For me, because I live out in front of myself, and often find it easier to give out than take in, working with the energy of my feet, legs, and back has been life changing. The practices that follow will help you balance your energy.

SHE WITH THE BIGGEST AURA WINS

There are big benefits, both spiritual and worldly, to becoming more intimate with your energy. The first is that we plug the bucket on our leaky energy. Second, we fill up our aura. Think of your aura as an egg-shaped energy field all around you, like a second body made of subtle energy instead of gross matter. Our aura determines our capacity to hold and circulate energy within and around us, as well as protect ourselves from the things we don't want to take into our field.

My mentor Cristal Mortensen once said to me, "She with the biggest aura wins." This means that none of the outer things we do in life matter if we are still constantly leaking energy. It's like walking around with a hole in our bucket. We leak energy by excessively thinking, worrying, working, or people-pleasing. We leak energy when we use our sexuality to feel better about our low self-worth. We leak energy when we aren't allowing ourselves to acknowledge and digest our feelings. We leak energy when we are more attuned to the emotions and energies of others than to ourselves. These are just a few ways. I'm sure you can come up with your own list. The point is, for most of us, learning how to pay attention to our own inner reality will begin to plug these leaks and give us more life.

Working with our energy also brings us into direct contact with our inner Divinity—our soul. We contact something both tender and transcendent, eminent and embodied. By working with energy, we realize that it is an infinite resource! It's all around us and inside us. As so many of the traditions say, there is "a father sky above" and "a mother Earth below." They are really great parents. They give great advice. They are always available. They will never leave us. And they are the ultimate source of energy for all of us! And as we learn to work with these infinite resources, we get better at letting other people (who are working through their own energy dramas) off the hook, and just get to enjoy them more.

Another side benefit of working with our energy is less fear of dying. Yeah, that little thing. Fear starts to dissolve as we connect to prana—something inside of us that *never* dies. Albert Einstein may have said it best: "Energy cannot be created or destroyed, it can only be changed from one form to another."

As we work with prana, the teachings of yoga say that we will begin to actualize more "good stuff." Not Ferraris and pay raises, but *real* rewards: our inner capacity for peace, bliss, deep joy, fulfillment, authenticity, willpower, right action, discernment, intelligence, and pure awareness. In this way, we learn how to energetically nourish ourselves, release the past, and move forward into a vibrant future. Your work is to fill yourself up with energy, *let it stay inside to heal and nourish you*, and let go of everything that isn't truly *you*. She with the biggest aura really does win in the end.

Okay, enough talking about energy, let's feel it.

⁎ A GLOW-WORTHY MEDITATION ⁎
The Back Body Waterfall

This is a practice I learned from my work with my mentor, Cristal Mortensen. Think of this practice as "home base"—it's a great place to start working with subtle energy.

In later practices in the book, we will learn to go into our bodies and to gather and hold more energy. But for now, let's start with a basic practice that brings in more down-regulation of the nervous system— something we all need. I use this practice when I feel overwhelmed or spaced out, or when the inside of my body feels way too intense.

*Begin by feeling the contact of the back of your body
or the soles of your feet on the chair or floor.*

Feel the weight of your body—gravity—and its contact with the chair or floor.

*Slowly, feel your attention moving from the front of your
body to the back of your body. Feel the texture, the weight,
and the sensations of the back of your body.*

*Then, bring your awareness to the top of your head. It may help to
remember the last time you were in the shower, or the feeling of being under
a waterfall. Simply imagine that flow of water moving down the back of
your head, the back of your neck, your shoulders, lower back, buttocks,
and down the backs of your legs, all the way to the soles of the feet.*

*Over and over again, gently and without force, let your
attention drop down the back of your body.*

*Notice the thoughts and feelings that come and go, but you keep
channeling your awareness to this waterfall-like flow.*

Back of the head.

Back of the neck.

Shoulders.

Lower back.

Buttocks.

Back of the legs.

*Keep repeating this downward flow cycle over and over. If it helps,
you can coordinate it with an even, easy rhythm of breath.*

*Over time, this may become an effortless flow of energy and attention. You
may also sense this back body channel opening up, allowing the mind to rest.*

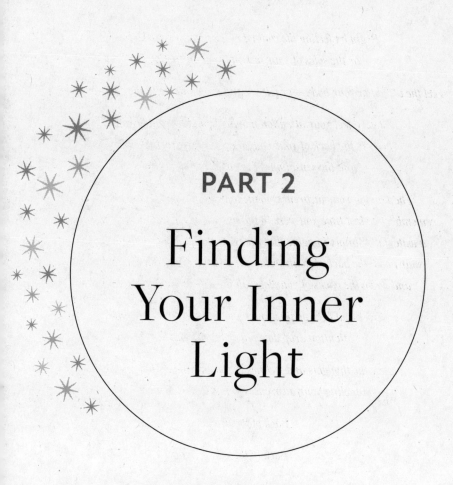

PART 2

Finding Your Inner Light

7

Intuition

The effect of working with our energy enables us to have better access to our true self and our deepest knowing around what direction we should take in our lives. Some call this deep knowing intuition. Intuition is one of the most important ways we can feel our connection and capacity for co-creation with our spiritual selves and our higher power. This chapter will walk us through the concept of intuition—what it is and what it is not—while the following chapter addresses the practical aspects of intuition, guiding us as we access this superpower and learn to hone our intuitive faculties.

I like to think of intuition as a connection point between the body and soul. Intuitive insights, I believe, are the way in which our highest spiritual self speaks to us in this human form, as if the God within us were giving us sage advice, different from the advice that stems from our temporary desires and habitual thoughts. In this way, intuition is both unique to you *and* a connection point to the greater universal intelligence within and without. And as we learn to hear it and follow it, we also feel more connected to who we really are and to the bigger divinity that holds *all of us* in this web of life.

Many times our intuition takes a backseat to the ongoing inner dialogue in our heads. It may be difficult to differentiate between our thoughts and our higher knowing. In this chapter, I will offer practices that help connect you to your deepest knowing by working with your mind and energy to find that still inner voice. We will explore techniques that will sharpen your intuition and help you not only access it, but live from it.

WHAT IS INTUITION, REALLY?

Intuition can feel like a premonition, gut feeling, or predictive hunch. It can also feel like a firm stillness, an inner security around a known truth. Examples in our world abound—the mother who somehow knows her child is being threatened and runs to their aid. The twin who can feel when her sister is getting sick on the other side of the planet. Or everyday intuitive magic like thinking of a friend and then they call. And while we all may agree that trusting our instincts is a good thing, we need to get really clear on what our intuition is and how to recognize its "still small voice" within the cacophony of everyday life.

Intuition is body magic. It is a basic part of our subtle anatomy and psychology. It needs no mental gymnastics or complex deliberation. It is a faculty we all share. Think of it as a combo pack of our animal instincts, felt sense (bodily awareness), and highest intellect. It is also the connection point between the conscious and subconscious parts of our minds. It is the ultimate high-functioning collaboration between the left and right brain.

People call messages from their intuition "hunches," meaning "shoves," because of their visceral immediacy. They are generated by the unconscious mind's capacity to rapidly sift through past personal experiences stored in the body, as well as the collective unconscious's cumulative knowledge. Consider intuition as the ability to know something immediately *with your body*, without the need for analysis. I've found that this hard-to-pin-down sense, when honored, is the most valuable body-based guidance system we have.

Your intuition comes from you, but it is also, according to perennial mystic thought, a part of the collective unconscious. What does that mean? It means you aren't alone. You are the result of thousands of years of ancestry and evolution, including their learning experiences.

From the Christian Gnostics to the Hindu Tantriks, the Shamanic Peruvians to the Zen masters of China, ancient mystics have always understood that our capacity for knowing things expands far beyond the limits of the individual, conscious mind. And the science behind intuition, which we will explore later, is catching up with what our traditional societies have known all along: So much of what we "know" comes from the unconscious self—from deep-seated processes in the brain and body that the conscious mind cannot access.

Everyone has the ability to be intuitive. Sadly, most of us are not taught how to do it, or even worse, it gets trained out of us as we are told the *one* right answer to every question in school. Our culture values the supremacy of the analytical and logical over the magical and visceral. And while our logical, reasoning capacity is a wonderful thing, it is only one part of our mind-body superpower.

Intuitive knowing is readily available in the body. It usually comes as a first sense we have about a situation. We feel it quite quickly through our body. It's the pit (or, sometimes, the gaping chasm) that you feel in your stomach, warning that something is "off." It's a sense of lightness and joy when you're in a flow state or around people who are true friends. It's a sense of being "lit up" when you hear about a new opportunity on the horizon. It can also show up in other physical ways, such as a sense of heaviness, brain fog, or buzzy energy (that's not caused by your triple oat milk latte!); even unexpected sleepiness could be your intuition speaking to you.

Along with these physical symptoms, intuition provides an immediate answer in your mind.

Stay away from that person.

This opportunity is energizing and full of potential.

This place is safe.

Don't go down that mental rabbit hole.

The problem is, we often discount both the body-knowing and the first-thought impression intuition provides. Why would we do this? For starters, intuition can be elusive. Sometimes that's because we aren't trained in our inner listening. Mostly, it comes down to the fact that *we don't trust it.*

Insight from intuition rarely fits neatly into our gold-standard means of gauging information: logical, analytical inquiry. In other words, we often can't fully grasp with our thinking mind what our intuition is telling us. It is important to mention that while intuition may sometimes go against our conscious, logical impulse, it isn't pure whimsy or emotional reaction. It dances elegantly and wisely alongside the rational mind, supporting it like a wise elder faculty inside. It is head in concert with heart.

Another stumbling block to heeding intuitive information is that it may not align with what others want us to do, or with the status quo. *Who am I to say this is a bad idea when everyone else seems to think it's great?* So, we discount the information and make excuses for our feelings. *I'm sure it'll be fine. I'm just being overly cautious because of my past experience with this kind of thing. I don't want to be a stick-in-the-mud.*

Think about your own experience: Have you ever decided to move forward on something—a relationship, a job offer, signing a lease—even though your *immediate* reaction was aversion? Maybe the guy charmed you, and you decided that your hesitancy was due to some past relationship drama. Perhaps the job checked just enough boxes for you to ignore the heavy, unhappy vibe in the office. Or the apartment matched your ego's idea of where you should be living by that point in your life, despite the nagging feeling that it'd be a financial stretch.

And then, down the line, you regretted your choice (hopefully without having to suffer too much!). When it became clear that you needed to change course, you were reminded: *I* knew *something wasn't right, but I did it anyway.*

An important aspect of intuitive knowing is that its guidance *goes beyond place and time.* The circumstances for the warning, or for the thumbs-up, *may not yet be in place.*

Maybe you *can* afford the apartment . . . until your company lays you off six months later.

The job *is* a good stepping stone for your career . . . until a management change has you working directly under someone who feels threatened by you, and it becomes miserable.

And the guy? Perhaps he's on his best behavior, "trying to change," when you meet. But over time, his old ways come back.

Your intuition knew it all along.

Ignoring intuition is particularly common for women—even though we have great access to this superpower! (Men have it, too, but for reasons we'll soon explore, women are natural intuitives.)

Why would we go against one of our most useful superpowers? Historically, a woman's worth was measured by her ability to please others rather than her ability to speak her heart and mind. And while it's great to be pleasing (just like it is to be pleased), the unfortunate insistence on being pleasant at all costs has a lingering legacy, causing women and girls today to struggle to speak their truth. We imagine what other people will think of us if we follow what our intuition says. Afraid of judgment, we course-correct toward the status quo. Sadly, our culture overlays our intuition with social norms, rules, and expectations. We will go against our deeper knowing to simply fit in.

Let me give you a very common example. When a woman is menstruating, she may get a signal from her body that she needs to rest. Instead of listening, she heads to a spin class because she is "supposed" to exercise every day. Then she plows through her endless errands. That night, rather than staying in and honoring her body's natural need for decompression, she heads to a social event for her partner's work. She couldn't possibly miss out, she thinks, especially for something as insignificant as her period. It would break the social and cultural norm that ignores bodily needs, especially periods, in favor of schedules and pre-laid, rational plans.

✳ A GLOW-WORTHY CONTEMPLATION ✳
The Intuitive Glow

Take a moment now to remember the moments in your life when your body perked up with a felt sense. Perhaps you received a clear warning or a deep knowing. What was going on in your life? What did it feel like in your body? Describe the qualities present in your body and mind as you received this insight. Perhaps symbols, omens, synchronistic events, and divine messengers played a part in you noticing something "special" being delivered through your intuitive faculty.

ACCESSING THE WISDOM BODY

You may intuitively sense that you are so much more than just your physical body. You have a mental, meaning-making, thinking self. An emotional self. An energetic self. And an intuitive self.

You might imagine having one body, but many layers. The Tantric tradition teaches that the soul is encased deep within these layers—kind of like Russian nesting dolls. Called *koshas* in Hindu philosophy, these layers represent physical, emotional, energetic, and spiritual aspects to our being. But rather than existing as separate atomized structures, the koshas coexist and energetically weave and flow into one another.

One of the innermost layers is called the *vijnanamaya kosha*, or "wisdom body." It is the layer of the inner teacher, the highest aspect of our mind, and the realm of intuition and insight. Accessing this layer gives us direct access to this wisdom body and, eventually, *through time and practice,* the experience of a sense of alignment and oneness with your innermost layer—the body of bliss. Yes, living more and more from our deep knowing opens us to a place of peace and joy that is beyond temporary happiness. Moreover, as we access these subtler layers of who we are, we become ever freer from the fears, seductions, and complexes we store in each of these layers and connect more fully to the heart, the center of our soul, and the resting place of our inherent and eternal bliss.

We cultivate access to the wisdom body by building *viveka*, or spiritual discernment—our capacity to discriminate between what's real and true from what's illusory. As seekers of our true self, cultivating viveka is perhaps the single most important thing we can do. This means making good decisions that catapult the soul forward.

INTUITION = BIOLOGY + SOUL: THE
SCIENCE OF TRUSTING YOUR GUT

Modernity has overvalued the intellect to the detriment of physical understanding and intuition. If we can't define something, measure it, or prove it, our reason-obsessed world simply dismisses it. Emotions and instinct, those messages spoken from deep within the mind-body, are often viewed as outbursts to control rather than as nudges to trust.

It is exciting to watch modern science finally catch up with ancient global mysticism, showing that intuition is *always* at work. In a study conducted at the University of New South Wales, researchers concluded that body-based "nonconscious emotional information" deeply guided decision-making.

In other words, it's not only the logical brain guiding us through life.

Another study, from the University of Exeter, found that gut flora—called the microbiome—also plays a role in decision-making, along with memory storage and mood. Researchers now understand that good bacteria in the gut make brain-derived neurotrophic factor (BDNF), a chemical that boosts memory and the formation of new neural connections, as well as serotonin, the neurotransmitter responsible for our sense of well-being. Dr. Emeran Mayer, a researcher at UCLA, describes intuition as possibly arising from both the microbiome and the vagus nerve, which acts as a whole-body information superhighway to the brain.

Scientists also hypothesize that our intuitive sense might be "located" in the hippocampus, as well as throughout our gut neurons—giving scientific credence to literally "trusting your gut" and explaining why good gut health may help us access our wisdom body and our spiritual discernment. I personally do not think our intuition is located in one particular organ of our body, but it is exciting to see science exploring intuitive insight as a reality.

KNOW WHAT IT IS NOT, TO KNOW WHAT IT IS

One of the best ways to access intuition is to know the voices inside us that are *not* it. It's simply not enough to say "Trust your intuition." Without self-reflection and self-knowledge, this (well-intended!) advice can lead people to say and do mindless things under the guise of "following their truth."

True self-trust comes from actually knowing *who* the Self is that you *can* trust. In Tantra, this is known as *vichara*, or the discernment to know who we really are and which part of us is in the driver's seat.

Just as there are many layers inside us, there are also many selves—
archetypes, if you will—living within each of us. These are the many aspects
or parts that together make up the entirety of our being. Some of these aspects
are young and needy, and some mature and resourceful. Some are generous and
some are scared and greedy. Some are sweet, and some not-so-sweet. Some are
on their way to light and some are really stuck in the dark. Some support the
bigger vision for our lives. Some are saboteurs.

Here are a few of mine: Wounded little girl. Bitchy teenager. Sexy manip-
ulative maven. Golden goddess people-pleaser. Hypochondriac. Control freak.
Catastrophizer. Trapped anxious baby. Perfectionist fixer. Victim, savior,
perpetrator . . .

Should I go on?

Now, while all these aspects of ourselves need to be welcomed to the party
of our human experience—they each play a role in our lives, after all—not all
of them should be making decisions for us.

You wouldn't let a fifteen-year-old decide who you should be dating, or a
nine-year-old choose your next big financial move. Similarly, when it comes to
making choices and decisions that impact your life in a big way, you really need
the wisest part of yourself at the table. This is intuition—the spiritual adult you
want in the driver's seat of your life.

By recognizing the influence of these many selves in our lives, we can deci-
pher intuition's voice by considering what it is *not*. Intuition is not vindictive,
grabby, or small. It will never steer you to harm yourself or others. Your intuition will never guide you toward addictive, reactive behaviors or old coping
mechanisms that aren't for your highest good. Simply put: If shopping is a
problem for you, you can trust 100 percent that your intuition is never going to
push you to buy a $500 sweater you can't actually afford.

Sometimes the New Age version of intuition is depicted as predictions we
make about the future, or fleeting feelings. But intuition is not reactivity. It is
not an excuse to constantly do whatever feels good to your ego. It's also not
avoidance and drama. Simply stated, true intuition is never wrong, and it will
lead to the highest and best outcomes for all involved, even if the results aren't
immediately apparent.

TRUTH TELLING DOES NOT MEAN
BECOMING A MEAN GIRL

So we now know that our intuition will rarely tell us to max out our credit card on Chanel handbags. It most likely won't urge us to give our second cousin a little more money for her drug habit. It won't tell us to binge on a whole pizza followed by a pint of ice cream.

Most importantly, being in your true intuitive self shouldn't turn you into a mean girl. A mean girl is not a woman standing in her bravery. A mean girl is the manifestation of a younger version of ourselves who is scared, angry, and reactive. Often, rather than making the time to take care of her, we react to the external circumstances that provoke her. We throw her out on everyone else. We want the world to change so she feels better. And it makes sense. She has often been hurt in the past, sometimes in brutal ways. But it is our task to use our wise-woman intuitive faculty to rein her in and grow her up so she isn't out there slinging shame-filled insults at other people on Instagram.

Recently, we have seen the cultural zeitgeist embrace the notion of "speaking our truth." This is a welcomed and much-needed liberation, especially for marginalized communities who have had their voices stifled and ridiculed for many years.

But the idea that *anything* we think and feel is somehow the ultimate truth is a notion worth reconsidering. The conflation of every reactive thought, emotion, and experience we have with "deep truth" is at best kinda annoying and at worst socially and spiritually dangerous.

How many times have you felt an overwhelming emotional reaction that felt super real in the moment, but then, when you calmed down, meditated, had a good cry, or got some more information on the situation—or maybe a new perspective from a wise friend—your "truth" changed? In the words of Mahatma Gandhi, "Truth is truth." It doesn't change on a whim.

There *are* occasions when our truths are *not* sweet and sappy. They can even be downright brutal to hear. But I have found that the more I rest in my heart's presence, the simpler my truths are and the more they can be conveyed with calm love. And even when they aren't easy for others to hear, the depth of my intuition gives me the words to convey them in a way that is kind and has less tendency to send others into a defensive position. More often than not, when a truth is conveyed in love—even if the words are fierce—others will be able to hear and digest it.

THAT TIME I REALLY SAID F-YOU TO MY INTUITION

I've been really lucky in my life to have a naturally strong intuitive sense. This is a blessing and a curse, because when you have a strong intuition, it is oh-so-bittersweet when you abandon it. There was one moment in my life that was so painful that I vowed to never go against my intuition again.

It all started with a man (surprise, surprise). The short version is that I met someone that I intuitively knew was a big NO. I could *feel* his lack of integrity and empathy. But he was tall, handsome, and had BDE (Big Dick Energy).

On the first date, he—without asking—put his hands all over me (red flag on the field). As I removed them, I asked, "So, what are you looking for in terms of women and relationships?"

"Oh," he responded, "I'm really not sure. I'm kinda just loving partying with beautiful people, doing lots of drugs, listening to electronic music, and just being free." (I am now swimming in a sea of red flags, because while these things may have been *his* journey, they were definitely not mine.)

At the end of the date, I politely told him that I was looking for something different than what he could offer me. I saw his face light up: I was challenging him. "Oh, come on, just come up to my apartment for a tea, and who knows, maybe I *do* want something serious," he said. (I am now drowning in red flags.)

My intuition started to whisper. "Go home," it nudged. "Take a bath. Love yourself. This dude is *Trouble*, with a capital T."

But my inner teenager *loves* danger. She even kinda likes assholes. "Oh, just go up for a tea," she said. "Have a little fun. You deserve this."

Meanwhile, my intuition was steadily urging, "Run! Run! Run!"

But I didn't run. I wanted to have tea. And tea I had.

Eight months later, I was on the other side of the most horrific relationship I will ever go through, a nightmare of codependent, narcissistic push-pull that ended in my physical and psychological health plummeting.

But keep hope, dear reader. Because, as so often happens, this heartbreak was also the greatest learning experience of my life. Years later, I even hold a feeling of gratitude for it, because it made me crystal clear on what I really want in a relationship, and how I was actually blocking that by letting my younger, wounded parts guide me.

It also gave me the opportunity to clear my inner space and open my intuition further by *forgiving myself* for betraying and abandoning my knowing. Most important of all, *I vowed to never doubt that inner voice again.*

I've hung out with enough women to know one thing: My intuition story is not unique. We have all had moments in our lives when we went against our heart's true knowing. We didn't listen. But we certainly learned some great lessons. In the next chapter, we will get better at learning to listen to that quiet inner voice and doing what it says. The next chapter will teach us how to then turn that deep listening into action.

8

Listening

Now that we've explored intuition conceptually, it's time to access it practically. This chapter will walk you through the "how" of accessing this important inner guidance system. We will see how truth, silence, presence, and "being in the body" are potent activators of intuition. We will also learn how to feed our mind good "food," trust our Divine Messengers, and deal with the inevitable pushbacks that arise when we are brave enough to stand in our knowing. Lastly, this chapter will help us navigate the tricky ground of differentiating our intuition from the constant chatter of thoughts that block our glow.

WHY IT HELPS TO BUILD OUR INTUITION MUSCLE

It can be hard to "hear" intuition over the endless stream of chatter inside our minds. Intuition speaks in subtle ways. It shows up each night for us in our dreams. It may arrive as a quiet knowing, a calm voice (usually—unless you keep ignoring it!), or body sensations that, if you're not tuned in, you might just dismiss. This is why priming your mind and body to notice these intuitive messages is so important.

We can think of our deepest intuitive faculty as the highest aspect of our mind. It is not the language of the ego or the intellect. It is the language of the heart and the result of being tuned to our subtle energy. Intuition speaks in ways that activate us on a cellular level and make us glow. It is always working toward the highest and best for all, and that includes you! We just need to listen to it.

The good news is that, like any other skill, the ability to hear our intuition gets stronger with practice. And the coolest part? The best exercises for building intuition also happen to strengthen self-esteem and *build your relationship to the Divine.* So, as you work on your knowing, you are also working on your very connection to God.

Why? Because *when you trust the whisper of your intuition, you are actually trusting God.* BOOM!!! (I know, my mind just got blown a little too!)

OK, let's dive into the "workout" for toning and building intuition muscles.

INTEGRITY BUILDS INTUITION

Nothing glows more than a woman who lives in her integrity. Integrity means our words, actions, and our truest inner self are all in alignment. And a part of building our intuitive capacity is cultivating that integrity.

This doesn't mean living a perfect life—just living from our realness. As we do that more and more, our deepest feelings, truths, words, and actions will begin to have a coherence to them. When we walk in integrity and use intuition as an integral part of our guidance system, it's as if our very body is emanating something true. This, again, is that inner glow, and we all know it when we see it!

I was overjoyed to learn that in Hawaiian culture, the word for integrity is *pono,* which is related to the goodness that arises from living in balance and harmony with ourselves, others, and the natural world that holds us. The ancient

Vedics called this important quality *aryavam*: letting your words, thoughts, and actions have integrity. And this alignment—*aryavam*, *pono*, integrity—is the spiritual equivalent of getting your shit together.

That's right—living in integrity is listening to the part of our inner Divinity that says, "Yeah, I love all parts of you no matter what, but get it together, woman!" It's the giddyup to your inherent lovability. It motivates you to make yourself better. But only *you* know what is right living for you.

Remember, this isn't about moralistic dogmas on righteous behavior. This is about living in alignment with *your* virtues, and from a place of wholeness and wisdom that speaks to your heart and your purpose in life.

Living in alignment is synonymous with being in your glow.

When you are in this alignment, you're more open to insight and guidance, whether from your unconscious (some say Highest) self or from a Divine source. The Vedic teachings call this transmission *bindu visarga*, which means "heavenly drop." And it's impossible to get those heavenly drops when we aren't living in alignment with our heart.

✴ A GLOW-WORTHY MEDITATION ✴
Waiting for the Drop

Take a moment to find a smooth, even ratio of breath.

Sense the movement of your ribcage outward and inward.

Feel an even ratio of breath.

Inhale. Exhale. Inhale. Exhale.

Be with this simple, even breath for a few minutes.

Then inhale . . . effortless pause.

Exhale . . . effortless pause.

Feel that insight and intuition that live in spaces between the breaths.

Staying with this breath of even ratio, gently pausing at the top and bottom of the breath, imagine a long line that runs from heaven above you, into your mind (thoughts), into your heart (feelings), through your belly (gut instinct, body wisdom), and into the groundedness of your Earth-based, everyday life. This line forms a bond of truth between what you think, say, and do and the earth and sky. Get quiet and sense that a heavenly drop is coming. Ask any questions and wait patiently for the answer to "drop" into you.

Remember to keep sensing the movement of your ribcage outward and inward.

Feel the even ratio of breath.

Then inhale . . . effortless pause.

Exhale . . . effortless pause.

Know that all of the answers to all of your questions sit in the place of effortless pause.

TELL THE TRUTH

It's easy to just say, "Speak your truth." But in my experience working with women, so many of us don't even know what our deepest truth is!

Is this my truth or the voice of my mother in my head?

Is this my truth or what the scared, wounded little girl living in my heart wants?

Is this my truth or society's truth?

Is this my truth or political propaganda?

IT ALL STARTS WITH THE HOLY PAUSE

We have to practice deeply listening to ourselves to begin to discern the truth from the untruth. And yes, here it is again. We need the Holy Pause, the first stage in attuning to our intuition is to remove all distractions.

✳ A GLOW-WORTHY MEDITATION ✳
The Inner Knowing

This is a deepening of the work we did in the last meditation.

Remember the Holy Pause. Take time to allow your attention to take in the outside world and the room you are in. Feel your body settle into the space.

You can also bring in the element of breathwork we practiced before. Try an inhale of 4–6 counts, gentle pause at the top of the inhale, and exhale out for 4–6 counts (making the exhale a bit longer than the inhale, and finding a gentle pause).

Call on your Divine Guidance if you want an even deeper intuitive connection. Ask your support for guidance in awakening your intuition and good decision-making powers.

As you relax, can you sense in your being a place of calm, presence, and maybe even love for yourself and the situation you find yourself in?

Now take a moment to remember a moment in your life where you just knew something very deeply. Feel that feeling of knowing in your body. Feel the wisdom, presence, and calm of that knowing in your body. Thank your body for this deep inner knowing.

From this place of calm presence, now ask the question or contemplate the situation that requires your intuitive knowing. Take some time here.

Wait for the answer. It usually comes quite quickly, but we often doubt it. It may come as a clear answer. It may come as a feeling. An emotion. It may be simple and humorous. It may say yes, no, or nothing at all. If there is no answer, the answer is usually, "Be patient, do nothing."

Trust what comes and have the bravery to act upon your deep knowing.

LET YES MEAN YES

It's not enough just to tell the truth when we are asked a question. We also need to get real about how we want to spend our time. And who we want to spend it with.

You see, nothing makes me happier than to help others. Seeing something I have said or done change someone's life is truly one of my own life's greatest gifts. But there is a shadow side to this desire to serve through love. Psychologist Terri Cole says it best: "Our culture rewards women for self-abandoning, codependent behavior."

If we say *yes* to friends, family, and romantic partners when we really *don't* want to do something, we are living in an energy that's inauthentic. What we say matters. Our words are actually deeply aligned with who we are. Let your *yes* mean *yes* and your *no* mean *no* to increase the power of your speech and strengthen your connection to your deepest, truest self.

This doesn't mean that we don't put others' needs before our own at times. There is a deep value in selfless service, in getting out of our own head and ego, and helping out the world by caretaking for our elders, making soup for our sick friend, or scrubbing our family's toilets. But our service should come from a deep understanding that service is the right path. Service should not come from a place of obligation, manipulation, or codependency, or be used as a way to avoid our own inner world.

The more we walk in truth and integrity—that is, the more we are aligned in body, mind, emotion, and spirit—the more power our words hold. You can witness the effect of this. As you increase your truth telling, your words will carry more potency and weight with them, and people will react to you differently.

By being in alignment and speaking your truth, you're tapping into your God-power. Speaking (and acting from) your truth also has a reinforcing effect, nourishing and purifying your energy. And this nutrient-rich energy is the offering you can then give to the world.

Lies, even the subtle or unintentional ones we tell ourselves, squelch our intuitive power. Tantra calls these unconscious deceits *vikalpas*. Think of a vikalpa as a false belief about the world that, while it may have helped you survive in the past, is now blocking you from your heart's deeper longing. And because they are so deeply subconscious, we aren't aware of how much they color our world.

If you're thinking, "No way, I'm not a liar!" you're likely lying to yourself! The thing is, we *all* lie, to some degree. There are even some cases where lying is necessary. But I'm talking about our inner world—where lying to ourselves (and sometimes to others) is how we turn our backs on our knowing. We often tell ourselves this kind of subtle lie instantly and unconsciously (which is why the Holy Pause helps take us to the truth *behind* our usual tendencies—it invites us to slow down and really feel what is true.

I know this relationship isn't good for me, but if I just hang in a little longer, it'll work out.

No, really, I'm not exhausted. If I can just power through this next project, my job will get easier.

Yeah, I know I shouldn't respond to this text until I calm down a bit, but I'm just gonna let it rip.

I'll give you an example of one of my whopper vikalpas. All my life I've wanted a soulmate. One day I woke up and asked myself a really tough question: Why do I *really* want a soulmate? The asking led me to a deeper truth lurking underneath: I wanted a partner so I wouldn't have to feel the painful feelings that arose when I was alone. The truth was I wasn't looking for a *real* partner. I was looking to stop the pain I felt in my aloneness. And denying this truth led me to relationships that ran the gamut of drama-rama to downright abusive. Now, I am clear on my deepest desire. I want a partner only if that person can contribute to my spiritual evolution, or at least not hold me back.

In order to be truthful with others, we have to be honest with ourselves first, and that can be hard. It means asking, *What feelings am I running from? Are there ways in which I am out of integrity? When am I not saying what I know to be true? Am I doing things that, deep down, I know are not what my true heart wants? Are there ways in which am I living out someone else's life or dream instead of my own?*

This is often an uncomfortable process, because we face the depths of our duplicity with ourselves and with others. Even if we can acknowledge that we haven't been honest with ourselves, it can be a lot harder to tell someone you love that you haven't been honest with them, even if that duplicity was unconscious.

But here's just one upside to finally being radically honest with yourself: It awakens integrity and juices up our glow.

And when we glow, we are sexy as hell.

So, speak your truth. Not on TikTok, but to yourself. To your spirit. Then, maybe, when you are ready, speak it to those who care about you and want to be in deeper relationship with your fine self.

After you recognize your truth, act on it. No matter what. The earned spiritual rewards *will* flow. It's your job to take care of your truth. It is the Divine's job to determine the timing and the way things need to show up in your life—to fulfill not the ego's longing, but the deeper desires of our hearts, a truth that maybe even we cannot see.

✳ A GLOW-WORTHY CONTEMPLATION ✳
Becoming a Truth Teller

Consider the following contemplations and feel free to write them out or say them aloud.

Am I hustling and burning the candle at both ends, pretending like I feel okay?

Do I really like the sex I'm having, or do I just lie back and do my duty? Do I need more intimacy? More time to reach orgasm? More sex? Less sex?

Am I really taking the time every day to tune into my heart and the Divine, or do I just talk about being a "spiritual person?"

Do I actually like my job, or do I secretly hate it?

Where in my life do I feel I am not living in full integrity and truth?

LISTENING TO YOUR INNER MESSAGES

Once, I was meant to get on an airplane from Virginia to California. I was feeling uneasy all morning, but my bags were all packed and the taxi was coming for me in ten minutes. Something in me said it wasn't just the normal pre-flight jitters. I decided to take a pause from my busy, get-ready-to-run-out-the-door morning. Something just didn't feel right.

I closed my eyes, put my hand on my heart, and silently asked, "Should I go on this trip?"

Instantly, I got a sick belly feeling, like a low-key gut punch.

It was a *really* annoying answer because it meant I had to cancel a bunch of stuff, let some people down, *and* lose money, but I decided to trust the feeling. I canceled the flight, the taxi, and my reservations. The very next day I got a call from my brother. My dad had had a heart attack and was in the hospital awaiting emergency surgery. I was so grateful to be close to my dad, rather than far away. I was glad that I didn't have to experience the stress of an emergency cross-country trip, not knowing if my dad would live or not.

While it was a tragic time, I was deeply moved by the power of my intuition to help me and grateful for that small but powerful moment when I stopped, put my hand on my heart, and listened to the feeling inside me.

The Holy Pause takes the place of the split-second, patterned, reactive decision-making process. Rarely is it a good idea to make a decision when you're freaking out. The Holy Pause is especially important when making big decisions with consequences. It will give you a clear yes, no, or nothing at all. If there is nothing at all, I interpret this as "wait and do nothing." When we are asked to wait, it may be because our timing is off. It may also be a warning to pause. Waiting and doing nothing can feel like a death-sentence to your ego! But I now know that it's a soul-level protection measure, and I trust it implicitly.

From this new less-reactive state, ask your intuition a question:

Should I be dating this person?

Should I be signing this deal at work?

Should I respond to this email right now?

Should I have another child?

You will usually get an answer instantly. It can feel like a warm honey heart-glow. It can also feel like a sucker punch. Be ready to experience some gnarly feelings when instead of going down your old paths (victimization, flirtation, addiction, compulsion, to name a few), you choose to listen to your heart. Your ego may fight your intuition hard, especially when it asks you to change. But with time, the old patterning of the ego will begin to loosen its control and give way to the quiet, calm knowingness inside.

The second part of the process is to trust that answer and follow its advice. This can be the hardest part. Why? Because *the truth of our heart often asks us to do very brave things.* Our intuition is always asking us to grow. It may challenge the status quo in our home. It may lead to upsetting someone who is used to us being a certain type of way. And that is brave work. But following our heart always pays off in the end.

GUT-KNOWING: ASK YOUR BODY, NOT YOUR THOUGHTS

Another way we can grow our body's intuitive sense is by paying attention to our body itself. This helps us orient our awareness toward something stable within, separate from the realm of thoughts and feelings. Getting a felt sense of your body in space, and the way it responds to stimuli, is helpful for tuning in and hearing what it has to tell you.

Another way to become more body-centric is to practice bringing your attention to your belly throughout the day—as you take a walk, talk to a friend, or run errands. Just notice how it feels in this area during these normal activities: spacious, warm, tight, agitated. You might be surprised by how aligned your "belly knowing" is to your circumstances! As you tune in to this storehouse of body wisdom, you might also become aware of how much time you typically spend in "head knowing" only.

You can also practice making a decision from your belly. Start by bringing your awareness to this area, and keep it there while you contemplate a decision, big or small. (You can place your hand on your belly if this helps guide your attention.) Wait for any shifts or changes in your belly—sensations of softness or tightness, of ease and expansion or of constriction, maybe a change in temperature—or for a gut-feeling to guide you.

SILENCE BUILDS INTUITION

Another practice that profoundly builds our faculty for deep knowing is building our tolerance for inner silence. Internal noise crowds out the voice of intuition. Overthinking. Overprocessing. A constant bombardment of outer stimuli that sends our brains and bodies into high alert.

Inner silence, on the other hand, is the fertile soil in which intuition, insight, and healing thrive. In many Eastern traditions, silence is considered the true ground of our being—a place in our mind of ultimate peace and calm. This true ground is a silence that exists behind our mental chatter. There's a good reason that monks and wise-women the world over have searched for quiet caves and meditation chambers. They were using outer silence to access the inner!

Anywhere can be your cave. For a lot of moms I know, their cave is a locked bathroom where they can hide for a few precious minutes in a bath-tub every night. For others, it's a backyard she-shed full of poetry and paints. When I was young and broke, mine was a little closet in my Oakland studio apartment that I turned into a "meditation room." It doesn't matter where it is. It just needs to be a reasonably quiet, private space. It can be deeply healing to find a few sacred moments of aloneness and silence each day. It is in this field of silence that we digest our life experiences.

Silence helps us become more attuned to the synchronistic, auspicious nature of life and bring a broader awareness to our reality. We can cultivate silence through meditation. It can also help to try taking a silent walk, drive without any music on, or do the dishes while *not* listening to a podcast. One of my favorite practices is to go outside in my backyard, where I have a comfy chair. I set a timer and just quietly look at the world, noticing what arises within me. At first it kinda sucks. Then something magical starts to happen. A deeper calm comes over me, as witnessing nature reminds me that there is a much bigger reality outside my head. My feelings of discomfort may still be there, but I can feel a bigger perspective emerging.

Another part of building silence into your life is lessening (or getting rid of!) negative inputs. These are the things that not only clutter your attention in the immediate present, but also feed a stream of thoughts and questions later on. Only you can know what those are, or how much of them you can tolerate, but a few possible negative inputs to consider include mind-numbing Instagram-scrolling, porn that demeans women, hyper-polarized news media, endless TikTok reels, or internet-stalking your ex's new squeeze.

Ask yourself: What is feeding and programming my brain every day?

Try this handy formula for reducing digital input: For every hour you spend online or otherwise engaged in an over-information download, take at least ten minutes of silence to digest it.

FOLLOW YOUR INNER KNOWING FOR A DAY

As we've noted, heeding what our intuition says is often one of the hardest parts of the process. At first it can feel like a risk to take the advice of this unfamiliar knowing. I advise starting with small decisions and practicing often.

Try acting from your intuition over the course of an entire day. For each decision you're called to make—*What should I wear? What should I eat? How should I respond to this email? Should I go to this event? Take this job? Sign this contract?*—use this formula:

1. Do the Holy Pause.
2. Find the pauses in your breath. Rest in those pauses, trusting that the answer lives there.
3. Ask the question on your mind.
4. Receive the answers, insights, gut feelings, and inner knowing.
5. Trust what is given.
6. Do what it says.

The more you do this, the easier it is to "hear" your body wisdom, and the faster the answers come. For me, the Holy Pause process takes less than a minute, and yet it often saves me a lot of time cleaning up messes from non–intuition based, reactive decision making.

TRUST THE DIVINE MESSENGERS

Our intuition may also come to us in the form of the outer world. I think of it as a Divine wink. Sometimes, it is a nudge. Other times, especially when I've ignored more subtle hints, God starts to yell. Intuition may appear as signs, symbols, powerful dreams—or Divine messengers, who can show up as people, animals, or sacred synchronistic occurrences. You don't need to follow, or even believe in, any faith path to be guided by the Divine signs. If it helps, you can think of the Divine messenger as your highest self.

Remember my story of the time I denied my intuition about a relationship and it bit me in the booty? What I didn't mention was that there were Divine messengers all around me, warning me about this person. People from the community seemed strangely compelled to share stories of his unsavory behavior with me. But because I didn't heed those warnings, God(dess) sent a complete stranger to make clear what I was dealing with.

I was at the airport and had stopped in a store to buy some snacks and reading material for my trip when the older man working the register looked at me, and in a thick accent said, "Young lady, I feel called to share something with you, if you are open to receiving it?"

I was taken aback, but ever the spiritualist, I nodded.

He looked at me with so much kindness that I felt tears come to my eyes, even before he spoke. "Don't let this negative influence in your life overtake you," he said, looking into my eyes. "Just know that *you know* what's best for your life. And you are meant to have a very different journey than the person you are worried about right now. You are a very special creature, and God has you in the palm of his hands. There is a negative influence that is attempting to take you off God's course."

Yeah, he said all that. An angel in a Charlotte airport.

In his kind gaze, I felt myself warm inside, a realm of timeless spirit enveloping me. Some deep part of me recognized this intervention for what it was:

communication from the spiritual realm. I sensed a halo of light surrounding both the cashier and myself, as time seemed to stand still. Tears streamed down my face as I thanked him and walked away, a bit in shock.

But a few weeks later, I was back in the bad relationship, totally ignoring my Divine messenger.

Don't get me wrong: At the time, I was consciously aware that each one of these interactions were Divine messages, and yet I still denied them. Some broken, deeply hurt part of me (yep, my little girl) needed to *really* learn that painful soul lesson in order to make me wake up and grow my sense of self-love. Like I said, learning to listen to your intuition is hard, and that is why practice is essential.

EXPECT PUSHBACKS

Another important aspect of building trust in our intuition is seeing pushback as a potential sign of progress. What does that mean? Well, as you begin to follow your intuition more, life won't suddenly get easier. It may even get harder. In fact, you should *expect* some negative feedback from the outside world as you trust yourself more and more.

Here's why pushback occurs: We all have certain relational patterns—the way we relate to the people in our lives. Some are supportive and helpful, and some are unhealthy or even codependent. When you begin to stand in your highest truth and integrity, the healthy relational patterns will likely grow stronger. The people who love you and support you and are on your team in every way will likely notice and respond positively. I think of these people as Divine Cheerleaders. When I follow my heart's knowing, my friends and colleagues are like, "Hell yes, woman." (These are the very same people that give me a little love nudge when my ego, not soul, is running the show.)

But as you start to live more from your intuition, some people will not be cheering. Every single way in which you are *not* in your highest truth and integrity may also become vibrantly apparent. Why? Because *growth*. And, by necessity, growth means *change*. Some people do not want to change, and they definitely don't want *you* to change, especially if you were paying their rent, washing their dog, or bankrolling their wardrobe.

As you start shifting your navigational system from old relational patterns that aren't in alignment with your truth to one that follows Your Highest Self Above All Else, others in that relation pattern with you are not always going to like it. It doesn't mean they're bad people; they're just used to the old you and your comfortable pattern!

When we begin to act from our intuitive integrity, from our highest truth, it can feel like walking in a strange new land.

I remember meeting with my friend Liz who was really upset because one of her yoga clients had crossed some pretty big boundaries with her. This client would text her all the time, all day long, constantly asking for health advice. This was really uncomfortable for her, because Liz is a genuinely kind person who wanted to help, but she felt a twinge of angst every time she heard the ding of her phone.

When I asked her what she *really* felt when she got all those texts, what she *wanted* to say that she couldn't, she immediately lit up, the rosy color came back to her cheeks, and she belted out loud, "Lady, stop texting me while I'm trying to make dinner and have sex with my man."

"Yes!" I responded. "That's your wisdom self!"

Now, Liz wouldn't want to say those exact words to her client, right? But what my friend was able to do, once she took the time to sit with her inner knowing, was craft a firm, kind response that stated her clear boundaries around yoga sessions, extra advice-giving, and getting texts from students.

What happened next was *really* important, and will likely happen to you, too, when you begin to step into your intuition. After expressing her new boundaries, Liz began to doubt herself. One moment she was this intuitive, empowered, and full-of-integrity boundary-setter (Glowy as Hell) and the next, a freaked-out little girl, afraid that she did the "wrong thing" and that someone was going to be mad at her.

"Maybe I shouldn't have said that!" she worried. "What if I hurt her feelings? What if I did something wrong?"

When I saw her recant, I smiled. Why? Because I knew my friend was *growing*. And I totally knew that feeling, from when my own truths had asked me to grow. Ouch!

Experiencing a sense of wanting to back away from an empowered decision may mean that you are "with" a younger part of yourself—a self that thinks they will get in trouble for setting boundaries. Or even worse, a self that thinks she will be kicked out of the tribe for standing up for herself. Creating healthy boundaries can trigger a whole host of survival defenses and false beliefs that may have aided us when we were younger but no longer serve us. It can feel like total *ick* to stay true to our adult self and its views.

Despite her fears, Liz was able to acknowledge that while it felt uncomfortable, it still felt *right*.

Then there was that other pesky lesson to learn: *that her student's reaction was out of her hands*. How other people will react to us when we are standing in our intuitive integrity is not our responsibility. But realizing we can't control the reactions of others can still feel really scary.

I'd like to tell you that the student promptly apologized for her boundary breach, and immediately signed up for ten extra sessions where she paid my friend for her valuable expertise. That did not happen. Actually, the client got pretty upset and decided not to work with my friend anymore.

But Liz was able to gather really important information from the end of her relationship with that student. She felt more confident and protected knowing that she didn't have to work with someone who couldn't respect her very basic and reasonable requests. She also was able to fill her schedule with people who *did* respect her boundaries and pay her for her valuable time and knowledge.

Even more importantly, my friend got to build a new relationship with herself, where the scared little girl part of her met the Big Mama part of her, the older, wiser Self who had her back. That is where real self-confidence comes from. As you begin to deeply feel when you are in alignment with your higher self's inner wisdom, and you speak and act from that place, others pushing back could be a sign that you are growing into a bigger, truer version of yourself.

HOW DO I KNOW IF IT'S INTUITION?

People ask me all the time, "How do I know when I'm in my intuition?" And my reply is always the same: *I don't know.*

An important part of your spiritual journey into the deepest level of self-trust and God-trust is learning to *know how you know.* What I can say is that I find the answers that come through my own intuition are often way more simple, compassionate, funny, wise, and patient than my ego's. And once you hone your intuitive faculty, you won't need to question why you know. You'll just know. You'll glow. And that feels freakin' holy.

So buckle up and hone your intuition because it will be your most trusted guide for what is to come. In the following pages we will encounter our shadows, wounds, and pain. I know it doesn't sound fun, but that's where the gold is.

9

Wounds

Everyone you meet is just like you in that we all have painful stories. And we all have experienced suffering. We've had our hearts broken. We've had our innocence lost or even taken. We've watched the way our lives didn't turn out exactly how we'd dreamed in the past. In other words: We are all, to greater and lesser extents, walking around with wounds. This chapter will ask you to consider these wounds as pathways to that eternal glow we all long for—as a way of revealing the soul.

THE DARK NIGHT OF THE SOUL: PAIN AS PORTAL

We've all had moments in our lives when it feels like God has abandoned us. I have had many an insomnia-laced night wondering if God was even hearing my prayers. And on those nights, I took comfort in the Christian tradition and the lives of great souls like Father Bede Griffiths, Hildegard of Bingen, Teresa of Avila, and Francis of Assisi, who each went through their own painful journey of mud-wrestling with God. I remembered their stories of anguish, disease, fear, and longing, and the way those prayers and petitions of pain softened their hearts into sainthood.

I once heard that Martin Luther King Jr. struggled with insomnia and often prayed to God at night. Thich Nhat Hanh's life path grew out of witnessing the horrors and violence of his war-torn country of Vietnam. Before the Buddha became enlightened, he was visited by a demon named Mara who threw every single fear and temptation at him for many nights until he finally became his full Buddha-self—or, to put it another way, awakened his glow! On the spiritual path, it is a well-known phenomenon: We all have to encounter, at some point, the Dark Night of the Soul.

What is more, our soul may have not one dark night in this life, but many.

I won't sugarcoat this: Working with the tough emotions, thoughts, images, and memories in our lives can feel like eating a shit sandwich. But life can either harden and embitter us, or take us deeper into the indwelling spirit of our heart. Most of the time it's easier to avoid the journey into our hearts—because that journey involves being present to what has been stored there, undigested. But enough pain may start to make us hungry for knowing what lies beyond our struggle.

Our methods for avoiding pain are limitless. In today's world, the numbing agent that is the internet provides a ready distraction. But beyond the web, there are endless substances that we can become addicted to—alcohol, shopping, exercise, drugs. . . even yoga and meditation can be ways of avoiding what we really feel.

I used to think of my own suffering and woundedness as a sign that something was deeply wrong with me. I felt like I had a flaw that no one else had. As I've aged, I now see that my perceived wounds and flaws are not unique. They are a reflection of my humanity. In fact, the parts of me I've always seen as problematic have been the very portals through which I have been able to encounter an aliveness and peace that I can only call "God." You may call it peace, awareness, or a divine awakening.

By bringing our magic formula—Presence + Love—into our wounding (and getting help from supports when needed), alchemy ensues. Our past wounds are transformed and transmuted into spiritual gold.

NEVER NOT BROKEN

The purpose of alchemizing our pain is not perfection. In fact, it can be incredibly liberating to free ourselves from the idea that we will ever be perfectly healed—the idea that we will ever *not* have a certain amount of discomfort and suffering in our lives.

I remember having my heart cracked open when I learned about the Hindu goddess Akhilandeshvari, *She Who Is Never Not Broken.* She is the keeper of the realm of hearts broken, dreams unachieved, and promises unkept. She is with us when we fall into a snotty ball on our bed, unable to keep the sobs from engulfing us. She is the opposite of "Move on," "Just get over it," and "Oh, come on, it could be worse." She allows us to be with our feelings until they naturally transform. She exists within us, constantly gathering the broken pieces of us back into her. And although she is always broken, her face is peaceful because she knows an important secret: that she is always there with us, coexisting alongside the pain. And *She Who Is Never Not Broken* is one of the biggest keys to accessing our true inner glow, in that she allows all the rusted, grimy, broken, roughed-up parts of us to be held in the warm gaze of her message: *You can be here.*

These double-edged goddesses teach us the beautiful and often painful lesson of the tension of the opposites. Can you embody these goddesses by holding the paradox of life, knowing that both brokenness and wholeness may always be operating in our lives?

✴ A GLOW-WORTHY CONTEMPLATION ✴
Pain as Teacher

Take a moment to think of a really hard moment in your life. Choose one that, on reflection, makes you realize you have come out the other side. Without taking away from how painful the event was, can you also see how it formed you into who you are now? Perhaps it built a level of compassion for others who have gone through the same thing. Maybe it gave you a

clarity of vision, confidence, or strength you never knew you had. Can you
see how those moments catalyzed the work you do in the world? Brought
in the right relationships? Awakened a passion for serving others?

We can think of *She Who Is Never Not Broken* as a helpful resource in the global era we live in—a time that the ancient Vedic tradition called the Kali Yuga, the Age of Darkness. This era is more than just a particular set of years. It is a state of being. During the Age of Darkness, we may feel the suffering, confusion, and disconnection that have always been aspects of humankind most acutely. In this era, we *know* things are out of whack. We see it splayed out in front of us in high relief. But the good news is that this time is also when it is easiest to find the light. Crisis and wounding offer two possibilities: harden and hide, or *soften and open to the reality of what is.*

It makes sense. When things are good in our own lives, that is rarely the time when we fall to our knees and offer up that most seminal of all human prayers: *Come Great Spirit, Be with Me.* On the contrary—when everything is going great in our life, we too often forget to call out to the Divine.

I often contemplate what my spiritual life would look like if I had the perfect body and the perfect husband and never felt sick or emotionally out of whack. I giggle as I write this because I can tell you that I would probably have a massive ego and not ever think about God in any shape or form. Plus, without having deeply known my own pain, I wouldn't really be able to deeply love others.

I like to remember what Thich Nhat Hanh said about the wounds we all feel:

> I could not like to go to a place where there is no suffering. I could not like to send my children to a place where there is no suffering, because in such a place they have no ways to learn how to be understanding and compassionate. And the Kingdom of God is a place where there is understanding and compassion; and therefore, suffering should exist.

SEEING ALL OF OUR FACES

One of my favorite myths from the Hindu tradition tells the story of a great love affair between the god Shiva and the goddess Parvati. Shiva falls in love with Parvati, but his love for her is incomplete. In this story, *she* becomes *his* teacher, revealing to him the true nature of unconditional love.

"Oh my sweet one, you are the most beautiful, fascinating creature I have ever known," I imagine him saying to her in the throes of a romantic moment.

"Shiva," she replies, shaking her head. "You cannot love me because you do not fully *know* me."

"Oh, but my beautiful one," he presses. "How can you say this? I love you to the ends of the Earth and through all time until infinity and beyond."

Parvati laughs knowingly. "Shiva, you can't really love me because you have not yet seen all of my faces."

"Show them to me," says the brave god. "I want to love you fully."

And with that, she rips off her face, revealing the wild, voracious Kali underneath. Her new face is withered and wrinkled. Her tongue is out, blood dripping from her mouth. In a split second she moves from a violent rage to a slumped-over depressive ball, skull and bones where her soft skin and fine garments once hung.

Shiva remains steady, witnessing her in her most ferocious form. He maintains his love-gaze and begins to make his presence bigger and bigger until he envelops her entirely in his loving arms. But he doesn't soothe her. He doesn't try to change her. He simply waits and holds her. He is unwaveringly *with her*.

After some time, her tornado subsides and she begins to melt back into the sweetness of his embrace, her face going from tormented and haggard to soft and kind. She is the beautiful, loving Parvati once again. She knows that Shiva has seen every side of her and she knows that his love is true. They are, in that moment, united in holy love for all time and forever more.

You are both Shiva and Parvati in this cosmic myth of holiness. And what this myth reveals is the immense amount of pure grit and bravery that it takes to actually stay with all aspects of who we are. In my experience (which is ongoing), it feels awful. My ego bucks and brawls. I feel defensive, angry, and terrified to see myself as anything other than the golden parts of me I prefer. Doing so, for me, often requires someone else holding up a mirror—calling up a trusted best friend, a sister, to get perspective, or enlisting a teacher, therapist, or coach to help me see those parts of me that my ego doesn't want to acknowledge. In this way, our ego is humbled and we are awakened to the love that rests behind all of our faces.

With time, and a lot of love, we start to trust that by not repressing the dark, scary, or unsavory aspects inside us, a new inner marriage can occur that makes us into an integrated whole. The bravery to see and love the worst of Parvati's faces required the courage of Shiva. But there is also courage in Parvati, who had the sheer lady-balls to reveal herself to him. She didn't hide and show him only her sexy, agreeable side. She trusted him enough to show him all of her.

WE AREN'T *REALLY* IN CONTROL

By seeing and accepting the less-than-great aspects of who we are, we can also begin to accept the less-than-great parts of our life. One of the deepest teachings of Buddhism is that everything is subject to change. There will always be things we don't like and things taken from us that we do not want to lose. Things we label as "the bad stuff" occur to all of us in this earthly life.

I remember hearing a saying: "God has often been found in prison cells and hospital beds." There is a tenderness that flowers in the heart when you realize that you are not in control of your life. Letting go, though scary, softens the heart, allowing Spirit to enter. As we sense our spiritual essence, the realization that something within us is bigger than our suffering, and more alive than dead, becomes possible. We are lit by a spiritual glow that reminds us of our immutable inner value. We can rest in the intrinsic goodness behind all our masks, strategies, and best-laid plans. *Agape, metta, nirvana, moksha.*

Wounds hurt. Pain is a neurological message that tells our brain where to focus the body's energy, allowing healing to happen. This is true both in the physical body and in our spiritual evolution. Without pain—without what we may consider negative emotions—healing is impossible.

In the end, it is Parvati's ability to release control, by showing Shiva *all of herself*, that allows her to feel the depth of his compassion. Being willing to let go is what allows the love in. That love helps the unintegrated emotions from our past be held and healed.

NOT RUNNING FROM THE DARK

There is a great story about a wise yogini sage whose son had died. One of her students found her sobbing unconsolably. "Teacher," the student said, "I thought you were an enlightened master, beyond the duality of good and bad emotions. Why are you crying?"

The wise woman responded, "I am crying because I am human. And I am sad." The teacher was doing the opposite of a "spiritual bypass," in which we disallow certain aspects of our true emotional experience. She was experiencing the rawness of her direct experience—waves of sadness.

Spiritual bypass is the repression of the brutal truth of life. It's sending all your "bad" feelings back down into the dungeon. It's pretending you are okay when you are not. But it's not just that. Spiritual bypassing can also look like an attempt to overly spiritualize or give a positive spin to situations that need to be grokked for what they are—painful and unpleasant. It can also be an insistence on immediately intellectualizing your experience, trying to think your way through your feelings. It often involves identifying with some of your emotions and not others. If you have ever said, "Oh, I'm just not an angry person," it may be a sign of denial, concealing an ocean of anger you are afraid of wading into.

Spiritual bypassing can also look like projection—always insisting that you are the good guy and seeing everyone else as the bad "other." It may also look like focusing obsessively on helping and healing everyone else in your life (a great way to not have to ever feel your own stuff). The bypass in its most insidious form shows up as seeing "only the good" in the world, denying the very real suffering, injustices, and horrors that exist. For many of us, it sneaks in under the guise of perfectionism: denying the reality that you are human and you have flaws, blind spots, and vulnerability is another very common way we bypass our spirit.

Simply stated, being glow-worthy does *not* mean we are above the experience of being a real human. In fact, the more we are attuned to ourselves and the spiritual realm, the more authentically we experience our humanity and the inevitable vicissitudes of life. The religious leaders who tell us we can simply give God all our troubles and live in a blissed-out wonderland devoid of any negative emotion do us a great disservice. Just because we believe Christ died for our sins or Buddha nature is infinite does not absolve us from the work of actually *becoming* Christ-like or Buddha-like ourselves.

And guess what?

We all spiritually bypass from time to time. But the more we open our hearts to who we are—the beautiful and the broken—the more we slow the roll of our ingrained spiritual bypasses.

UNCOMFORTABLE EMOTIONS ARE GODDESSES

Think of the pain of life and our darker emotions as Goddesses in disguise. If we know how to feed these Goddesses and give them their due, they become strengths and gifts. If we don't work with them, they silently wreak havoc on our lives.

Pain and emotional upheaval are messages and warning signs. Suffering is a call from the soul to wake up. Our wounds can guide us back to the unattended, lost aspects of who we are. In the emotional realm, the darker emotions of fear, shame, anger, and sadness take us straight to the most wounded parts of ourselves, the ones that are still unintegrated and in need of healing.

In this way, we can think of our emotions not as something to kill off, but as divine gifts inviting us into a deeper relationship with the unknown parts of ourselves. Being totally present to all aspects of our experience allows us to be filled with the power of our previously unintegrated emotions. By giving them our presence (without totally *becoming* them), we build that new superpower we've been working with this entire book—loving presence.

In this way, pain, suffering, and our most wounded aspects can become holy potentialities leading us toward our inner light. It is that light that makes us glow. And we are all worthy of experiencing that glow, just as we are. By viewing the various forms of pain, imbalance, and brokenness within us as *forms of unintegrated divinity,* we can radically alter our perspective on our struggles. We see our wounds as painful gifts that can catalyze our becoming more connected to the truth of who we are: She who is never wounded. *She Who Is Never Broken.*

So many myths and mystical practices from the world over speak to the seemingly paradoxical nature of boldly facing our darker emotions as transformative spiritual work. Ancient practices and modern Western psychotherapy often invite us into an intimate relationship with our darker tendencies and fears. Some of these practices even refer to this work as "feeding our demons"—allowing the nectar of our loving presence to transform them into allies rather than enemies.

The question we may want to ask is this: How can we, in a way that feels safe and slow, open the door to the most shunned and discarded parts of ourselves? How can we begin to integrate our shadows? If we are feeling the so-called negative emotional aspect of ourselves, particularly those emotions that feel disproportionate to or disconnected from our current reality, it is almost guaranteed that we are working from an old wound that has not been fully healed or a shadow that has been banished from the Garden of What Is Acceptable to Love. Our emotions and life challenges are often cries from our own deepest heart asking us to put down our to-do list. "Please, come and get me," these emotions say.

I want to give you an example from my own life. For much of my thirties, I was single. I lived alone and I traveled a lot for work. When I arrived home from long trips, I would feel an inevitable sinking feeling in my heart and belly as soon as I walked in the door. It felt like a deep, constrictive dread.

Instead of taking the moment to feel that and be with the discomfort and pain, I would rush around unpacking, sorting mail, and otherwise staying busy. Then, when the exhaustion from the trip sank in, I would order a ton of takeout and sit down in front of the television. Now, there is nothing wrong with sorting mail, ordering takeout, or vegging out in front of the TV. But in my case, what I really needed was to stop and feel the emotion *behind* the need for TV and takeout.

One day, I decided to try something different. As soon as I came home, instead of just automatically rushing about, I stopped and looked around my house. I let my body and soul actually *arrive* in the safety of my familiar space. I put my hand on my heart and I did the Holy Pause.

Putting your hand on your heart may *seem* simple. But it is not. It is a miraculous gesture, often used by spirit-seekers around the world. Putting your hand on your heart brings you out of your head and into a form of body listening. By bringing your hand to your physical chest, your attention moves automatically from the head downward. The heart *knows, interprets, and conveys* information back to your mind in a way the thinking brain cannot. Moreover, the physical touch of you-to-you immediately augments your sense of being safe.

A few seconds after putting my hand on my heart, I realized how afraid I felt. As I sat with that, the fear began to melt into a deeper sense of sadness. I let the lonely sadness swirl around inside of me, and treated each visiting emotion like a sacred guest. As I felt them, something else emerged: a loving awareness that began to acknowledge and envelop the sadness. Soon the awareness became bigger than the sadness, causing the tension and resistance surrounding the feeling to burst like a bubble and release.

The sadness was not gone fully or forever, but what remained was surrounded by something that felt protective. I didn't feel as alone. I felt accompanied by something gentle and wise. It was bigger than me, and simultaneously it *was* me. The wound of loneliness had taken me to the gift of pure presence. At that moment, I knew I was not alone anymore. Sure, loneliness is an emotion I still feel, but I know that there is something else inside me beyond that lonely feeling. And if I explore it, and give that tender vulnerability a little time, it can take me even deeper into myself and my sacred light.

FROM COW DUNG TO HOLY ASH

I want to repeat something important: Working with your emotions is hard. It can feel like being dropped into a fire—you just want to jump out! Remember, this is that intermediary feeling of eating a shit sandwich that often accompanies becoming awake to everything we've sent to the Dungeon of the Unacceptable. In other words, Parvati does not transmute into her truer self immediately after she has revealed her ugly face. She must first wait for Shiva to see her. We have to be patient with our emotions. We have to hold them without wanting them to be different. That's the secret sauce!

In Vedic rituals, *vibhuti*, or "holy ash," comes from the alchemical process of burning cow dung. Cooking the dung transforms it into a sacred substance that is applied to the "third eye," a symbolic space between the eyebrows. What a beautiful teaching, and an important reminder that sacred wisdom can emerge from even the most reviled, taboo substance on the planet—literal shit.

As we become more integrated, we feel the full spectrum of our emotions more. But when we learn how to digest these emotions through our presence and love, eventually they come and go quite quickly. This process takes longer if there is long-standing trauma or a repeated self-defeating narrative. According to legend, the Buddha laid it out succinctly: "The arrows of emotion hit me once, they hit you a thousand times." Where the Buddha witnessed his raw emotions without getting caught up in a story about what they mean, we get entangled in *thinking* about our feelings rather than just experiencing them. We craft elaborate meaning and stories about them. We even call up our besties to retell the stories behind them over and over! This keeps us in a pattern of being hit by emotional arrows.

The more we trust in our inner light, the more we have the authentic emotional experience of being human. Ironically, the more we make room for our chaotic feelings, without judging them or projecting them onto others, the more grounded, stable, resilient, and peaceful we become. We expand the banks of our emotional river, which allows us to hold more of ourselves and more of the world.

JUICING YOUR MANGOES

Healthy emotions are energy in motion. When they are witnessed and allowed to move without judgment, they digest on their own. But instead of allowing this movement to happen, many of us tend toward emotional repression. This can look like numbing out, eating/drinking/shopping away our feelings, refusing to feel certain emotions, denying our feelings, and avoiding emotions in general.

At the other end of the emotional spectrum, we might spray our feelings on everyone else through angry outbursts, casting blame, or dwelling on the perceived flaws and crimes of others. Often, our emotional volatility is actually an expression of an unconscious desire for others to digest our emotional reality for us. We see this all the time in the consciousness desert that is social media, where those with the most internal turmoil post the most heinous commentary.

None of these coping mechanisms will lead to actual emotional digestion.

How do we digest an emotional experience? We pause. We allow the feeling to exist. And we observe it, in the body, as a felt sense, without judgment or condemnation, and without wanting it to be healed, different, or gone. We let it be pure and raw. Pulsing and moving. We cease to give it a meaning or a story. We are with it. *We do not identify with it and treat it as who we really are.*

Digesting emotions can be incredibly challenging in the moment, and it doesn't feel good initially. It's common and normal to not be able to handle our emotions on our own, and when this is the case, it's a good idea to call a trusted friend or therapist for support.

When and Where to Get Assistance

We want to work with our emotions in such a way that we don't merge into them and get swallowed up. If you feel you are over your threshold, take a walk, call a friend, or watch a funny show. More importantly, there are many deep wounds that really shouldn't be rewired alone (attachment issues and trauma, for example). These things should be worked with under the guidance of a good teacher, therapist, or mentor. Please consult the resources section for additional support.

We can work with this emotional digesting in a more basic way by going straight to the heart of our emotional body.

Vasant Lad, one of my favorite Ayurveda experts, says that working with emotions is like eating a mango. To really get the full benefits of the mango—its full nectar and sweet juiciness—we have to wait until it is ripe. Simply analyzing our emotions with our mind, without feeling them as raw, embodied energies, is like trying to juice an unripe mango. There is no transformation and no nutrition. Life is less sweet.

The moment to be with our experience is when we are *actually* in the emotional body. In other words, the best time to digest our old emotions—to juice that mango—is when we feel an emotion arise. Alternatively, we can actively call up an uncomfortable memory to get us in the felt experience of the emotion. The following practice will help you allow the emotions to flow and the sweetness to emerge.

✳ A GLOW-WORTHY CONTEMPLATION ✳
Juicing Emotional Mangoes

For many years, I worked with a body-emotion focused psychotherapist named Barbara Gabriel. She taught me a form of emotion processing that brought me out of the intellect and into the somatic experience of my emotions. We called it an "emotional wash-cycle." And instead of waiting on our life to give us a whopper of a feeling that stops us in our tracks, we take time throughout our day to feel any little (or big!) feelings that may have built up beneath the surface of our awareness. I've outlined the basics of the process here:

When you are feeling a strong emotion, try not to judge yourself. We all have these feelings from time to time. Know that it will pass. It can help to name the emotion, and to notice the feeling of the emotion in your body. You can say the words aloud or journal them if that feels better for you.

What do you feel angry/sad/afraid/ashamed/guilty about? Rather than focusing on the content, focus on the feelings that arise and try to witness them without judging.

Once you have identified the emotion, let go of all names and stories. Simply notice the pure, raw experience of the feeling. Where does it live? Does it have a temperature? A texture? Without words and stories, what is it like? Keep a loving presence around whatever you are noticing.

WITNESSING FALSE BELIEFS

When we work with our emotions, we tend to find the same old false beliefs beneath the body's emotionally reactive holding patterns. False beliefs are out-dated stories, usually formed when we were young (or from past lives, if you wanna go deep!), that aren't true or reflective of our current reality. They lead to particular expectations for ourselves and others and can also act as self-fulfilling prophecies that attract scenarios that "prove" their "truth." And while we all have a unique set of triggers that make us feel the hurt, when we follow our deepest pain down to its core, it all tends to boil down to similar beliefs and feelings about being unworthy, unwanted, or alone.

By bringing these ancient stories and feelings to light, we can begin to see them with compassion. With compassion, old beliefs and feelings often dis-solve and change, reflecting a new mindset that is here now. We become awake to a truer perception of the present moment that is more mature and not based on the past. Our hearts can open again.

$\ast \ast$ A GLOW-WORTHY CONTEMPLATION $\ast \ast$
Heart-Constricting Beliefs

When you get to the root of your emotions, what beliefs are there? Do you really believe these stories? Or are they the beliefs of a much younger you?

Here are some of the most commonly held heart-constricting beliefs. Notice if any resonate:

I am not worthy of love.

I am fundamentally flawed.

I'm too young/old.

I'm not good (smart, beautiful, skinny, cool, rich, etc.) enough.

I will not be successful in my endeavors.

I am alone.

No one else feels this way.

Things will always be this way.

No one will ever want me.

If I'm not perfect, I'll be punished.

As you allow the old beliefs and feelings to move, what else is true?
Are there any positive emotions emerging from underneath the pain?
Is there any new clarity on how these old stories may have been true
in the past but aren't anymore? Or maybe have never been true?

Is there a new sense of something else being able to hold all of you, both
the positive and negative parts? Have your beliefs about your story
shifted now that you have digested some of the old pain? Have any
insights emerged from your more awake, compassionate, adult self?

LEAVING HOME

Sometimes our old wounds and past experiences can make us feel like our own bodies are not a great place to live. Exercise, yoga, dance, massage, and other forms of movement and body work can be incredibly helpful in allowing us to reinhabit our bodies. But sometimes these practices cause us to become hyper-focused on our bodies, without necessarily helping us feel more at home there. This is a subtle but important distinction. What is more, you can do all the "right things"—movement, mantras, sauna, ice baths, herbs, biohacking, etc.—but if you can't be present with who you really are inside your body, these techniques will take you only so far.

The question is, why do we leave our bodies? And how can we come back home?

The reason is discomfort—we do not feel at home inside our own skin. This discomfort has taken on different names throughout time: trauma, karma, core vulnerabilities, or just the human condition of suffering. We may think of trauma as something that happens only to victims of war, natural disaster, sexual assault, or other forms of violence. And those things can definitely be traumatizing. But research shows that some people go through those horrifying events and come out untraumatized, even as others are deeply impacted and suffer. This doesn't mean that the people who came through untraumatized were stronger in some way. It just means that what is traumatizing for one person may not be for another. "Big" traumatic events are important, but so are the smaller but still impactful traumas people suffer when going through everyday human losses—a bad breakup, parents divorcing, job loss, or the death of a loved one.

> *"Trauma is not what happens to you. Trauma is what happens inside you as a result of what happens to you."*
> —Gabor Maté

Trauma is both individual and collective. It is the unmet needs of our birth, infancy, and childhood. The heartbreak, addiction, and abuse held as secrets inside families. It is the thing that can never be fixed, only transformed. Trauma is inside all of us, and it longs to be witnessed.

Moreover, in most of us, the body and mind have a negativity bias. This means we dwell on memories, emotions, thoughts, and sensations that remind us of all the bad stuff that has happened—or could happen at any moment—rather than the good stuff in our lives.

Each of us carries around an unacknowledged storehouse of our deepest wounds—painful past impressions that, to protect ourselves, we have made prominent in our memories in hopes that we might avoid ever experiencing them again. And these stored memories are constantly influencing our present perspective. We can think of trauma as being like the Vedic tradition's negative karmas: traces from the past that act like hungry ghosts, "haunting" our experiences.

We all carry these karmic overlays in our nervous systems. We create our own overlays when we become caught in a constant loop of reliving the past. But these overlays may also come from our parents and their own relationships to their bodies, the media, the medical world, social and religious institutions, or any other person or system that tells us how we should look or who we should be.

AN OLD STORY: SOUL LOSS AND RETURNING HOME

We think of trauma awareness as an emergent modern phenomenon, but this is not the case. Trauma's impact on us was well known in the shamanic traditions, which referred to trauma's effects on our body and mind as a soul loss. Things get to be too much inside the body, so the soul decides to leave for a bit.

Shamanism is the original form of sacred healing—a vast array of traditions and practices found in nearly every society on our planet. It is our oldest form of psychotherapy, medicine, and religion. In this art and practice, the body, mind, environment, and unseen world are in deep relationship. Medicine and spirituality are not seen as totally separate but instead as connected layers, each influencing one another in the unseen realm. And a central practice of these spiritual medicine practices was soul retrieval, or ancient trauma-release.

The essence of soul medicine was the idea that throughout our life (or even lives), the hurts, losses, accidents, and relational entanglements we all experience leave grooves in our soul's memory. Whenever we store away a memory inside (often in an attempt to just move on), rather than fully digesting it, a small piece of our soul (or prana) departs from the body. This is a soul loss—a fragmentation of the soul's energy.

In modern Western terms, we can think of soul loss as dissociation, or what happens in the nervous system when we experience the freeze reflex. Dissociation is not necessarily a bad thing. Freezing is a natural and healthy tool our body uses to survive. On a psychological level, dissociation is a prerequisite for daydreaming and using our imagination. But if you find you are often living in a daydream, experience constant brain fog, or simply get stuck in your thoughts, this can be a sign of too much dissociation.

Dissociation is a lifesaver for us when we are in a traumatic situation where we cannot deal with what we are experiencing. We can think of this soul-ejection as being a blessing for our younger or past selves who, at the time, simply could not emotionally endure a traumatic or extremely stressful experience. It's as if our soul has an innate protective wisdom that knows how to shield us from the psychological and emotional overwhelm of experiencing the fullness of our suffering in the moment. But at some point, the whole of our true selves must return to the body to be reintegrated.

Soul loss can range from a vague sense of not being fully in the room to more intense forms of leaving reality. I've known my fair share of dissociation—from insomnia and addiction to just the feeling of being awkward in social situations. And I know many women who tell me they have to leave their body just to have sex with their partner. Dissociation can also show up as "living in your head"—overthinking, ruminating, and having obsessive thoughts—or as feeling spacey, brain-fogged, numbed out, or lethargic, feelings that cause an inner distrust around our ability to complete tasks.

We may also hold a feeling that a part of us is just fundamentally messed up. I notice it in myself as a longing or nostalgia for a connection that feels lost. You may feel it as insecurity, a lack of personal power, chronic worry, sadness, an inability to speak up, or a sense that life doesn't have a deeper purpose. These are all examples of a potential soul-ejection situation.

Through learning how to be lovingly present inside our physical bodies, we can guide the soul to return. And while the benefits of returning our true selves to our body are immense, I want to emphasize that this "coming home to the body" is often a slow process and should not be rushed or taken on alone. There is a reason that a guide is present in traditional spirit-medicine journeys. As the soul returns, many of the raw, original emotions that could not be processed in the moment arise and need to be digested by our adult selves in the present. This is an unavoidable step in the healing journey. But the ancients saw this as a temporary part of the return, calling it "purging," or release of the original imprint. Keep in mind that retrieving one's soul can take many, many years. It may even be helpful to think of the process as a lifelong journey of retrieving lost pieces of ourselves as we purify ourselves of old memories, false beliefs, and reactive emotions.

Although the healing of wounds is often accompanied by pain, the benefits of this courageous soul-medicine are vast. Returning to our body allows us to feel the earned reward of feeling that we belong to ourselves and our lives. We start to feel energized by our raw emotions instead of constantly pushing them down. We live with a deeper sense of courage and self-esteem because we now know that pain in life is a part of the deal, but we now feel we can endure our experiences. We are not only better able to recognize our inner light, but feel worthy of its glow.

Being back in our body with access to the full spectrum of its power and life force leads us to feel more energized, radiant, and vital. The joy of having our true selves fully inhabiting our bodies brings unlimited potential benefits, including improved stability, calm, resiliency, willpower, influence, choice-making, intuitive capacity, and physical health, as well as the ability to stand in our true power. Most importantly, we no longer look to other people or the world to be our "safe space." This is because we now feel safe within our own self, and know this is our true refuge. We learn that we can tolerate even our most difficult feelings. We are, more and more, inside our own soul. We become weatherproof.

PRACTICAL SOUL RETURN

We now know that it is not enough to simply be aware of the feelings and sensations inside our bodies. We need to infuse the experience of being in the body with *Presence + Love*. It can also be very helpful, especially when we are feeling overwhelmed by our emotions, to call in our higher power, or connection to the Divine. There are also methods and practices that can help create a channel through which the soul may return and feel more at home in the body. These practices help reestablish a sense of self-generated safety and belonging within us and build on everything we have already been practicing in this book.

Connecting to Support

Remember, when dealing with trauma it is very helpful to have relational guidance. In fact, in my experience, it is *required* for situations where inner sensations, memories, and thoughts feel overwhelming. Please make sure to reach out for support from a therapist, spiritual counselor, or coach when working with material that feels traumatic. Consult the resource section for more information.

✳ ✳ Ten Practices for Inviting the Soul to Return ✳ ✳

1. Hum or sing. You can also chant the sound *vuuuuuuu* three times. Feel it in your body as you chant and then take a moment after the chant to notice the effects.

2. Take a few minutes throughout the day to orient yourself to your environment, either outdoors or in whatever room you find yourself. Pay attention to the colors, shapes, and textures of the everyday objects in your external world.

3. Feel gravity. If you are sitting, feel the weight of your body in the chair. Really notice how wonderfully heavy your butt and legs are. Feel the sensation of your back and shoulders against the chair.

4. Do some skin brushing with a brush or loofah, or give yourself a good self-massage.

5. Press your fingers into your arm bones and feel the skin as your boundary. Simply bring one hand to the opposite arm. Press the hand into the bone and feel the bone press back into your hand. You can also do both arms at the same time. Keep your awareness on bringing yourself back into your bones.

6. Get grounded. Go outside, take off your shoes, and feel the contact between the soles of your feet and the earth. Do the grounding meditation on page 81.

7. Let nature be the object of your attention. In the words of author and scientist Gregg Braden, the glow that we experience while communing with nature "harmonizes the unsettled and fearful emotions of the mind. Shifting our attention from the chaotic matters of the world to the harmony that's reflected in nature and the human body frees us from fear and suffering."

8. Meditate on the downward flow. Return to the meditation on the waterfall of energy from page 81. This one is particularly great for feeling inner safety and coming home to your body.

9. Call in Divine guidance. Once you feel that you are better ori-
   ented on the earth and inside your body, ask your spiritual guidance to be with you in your practice of returning. Refer to the
   practice at the end of this chapter for some easy steps for calling
   in sacred support.

10. Get help. You aren't alone in this. We *all* need healing. If money
    is an issue, there are resources at the back of this book that can
    support you. The money I have personally invested in this type of
    support has given me back a sense of myself that is more valuable
    than anything else I could buy.

A GLOW-WORTHY MEDITATION

Coming In and Down

Remember our original energy practice—the one on imagining that
back body waterfall (page 81)? That is the practice to go back to
when you need to soothe and calm your nervous system. Once you feel
settled into that practice, however, you can build on it with this one,
allowing yourself to come in and down your body. Think of it as practical soul-return. Again, it is based on my deep mentorship work with
Cristal Mortensen.

*Begin by feeling the contact of the back of your body
or the soles of your feet on the chair or floor.*

Feel the weight of your body—gravity—and its contact with the chair or floor.

*This time, bring your awareness to the top of your head, but rather than
going down the back of the body, we will travel down the middle of the body.
Feel your attention and energy drop down from the top of the head, through
the middle of it. Now, down through the throat, heart, belly, abdomen,
and down through the legs. All the way down to the soles of your feet.*

It's that simple. Over and over again, gently and without force, let your attention drop down through the middle of your body. Like a flow.

As you do this, it's important to sense that the essence of who you are is what is coming in and down. Feel that the essence of you can really inhabit your head. Throat. Heart. Arms and hands. All throughout your belly. Sexual organs. All the way down through your legs, right to the bottoms of your feet.

Feel like you can bring your full presence all the way down into you.

If it helps, you can also add the element of breath. As you inhale, feel the flow down the middle of you from your head to the back of your heart. As you exhale, feel it continue to flow from the heart to the soles of your feet.

Over and over again, inhale down from the head to the heart, then exhale from the heart to the soles of your feet.

Notice the thoughts and feelings that come and go, but keep channeling your awareness in and down through your body.

Remember, if any of the sensations are too intense, simply return to the back body meditation we did before.

WOUNDS ARE STICKY

When we learn how to feel more at home in our bodies, we are better able to face our inner wounds. We begin to gain confidence in using our past pain to deepen our spiritual life. But it's important to remember that *wounds are sticky*. They suck us in, and we begin to identify with them. We may unknowingly continue to give our old wounds our power. We may use them to manipulate others.

Simply stated, bringing our pain to the surface is healthy. But rolling around in that pain over and over again keeps us stuck and can cause us to live in an eternal victim mentality.

So, how can we work with our emotions and trauma as portals into the Divine without getting stuck in the wound?

The key in working with our wounds is not to merge into them, even as we practice seeing them and feeling them with loving presence (and trust me, merging into them can be very easy). For example, identifying with a mental health issue can be liberating at first. It's a wonderful thing to destigmatize the anxiety and depression so many modern humans are dealing with. But wearing our mental health status like a new identity and badge of honor will only deepen the groove, causing us to merge with the very pain we are attempting to liberate ourselves from. The point of working with wounds is to *come out of them*.

Rather than constantly draining your life force by talking about how big your problems are, give your demons their due. Take time out of the day, feel your feelings, and listen to what they are trying to tell you. Then spend the rest of the day in praise and blessing (which we will get to in a later chapter—hallelujah!).

When I am working at confronting my shadow, a vision of the goddess often comes to me. In one hand she holds her shadows and pain. In the other hand she holds an infinite matrix of love and support. She can contain both. She needs the braveness of spirit to confront the darkness of pain as well as the love and nurturance to actually digest it. Things get polarized and messy when we *only* see pain, or when we bypass straight to positivity and disallow the pain.

WOUNDS CAN POINT TO DESTINY

The good news about all this pain is that facing it and working to integrate it can lead us to our highest destiny, or *dharma*. Dharma is the highest expression of our life journey. It is who we are meant to become, and how we are uniquely meant to show up in the world. It's acorn, meet oak tree. It's a calling. It's real authenticity. And it is our Divine destiny.

Dharma is also the beauty that comes from being completely ourselves—completely in alignment with the Divine and acting from that place of alignment. We live our dharma when we serve the world in a way that isn't burning us out or being used as a distraction from our pain. Dharmic living is when we feel like our life has meaning. As psychiatrist and Holocaust survivor Viktor

Frankl writes in *Man's Search for Meaning*, "The greatest task for any person is to find meaning in his or her life." The ancient Vedic Purusharthas teach us that if we don't feel a meaningful sense of connection and contribution to our community and our own evolution, *we will not be completely fulfilled*. And I don't know about you, but I want complete fulfillment.

In my own life, I know that some of my happiest moments have been when I have been both deeply connected to myself and in service to others. I feel an irresistible sense of connection as God works through me for the benefit of all. Your dharma doesn't have to be big and flashy. It may not make you uber-famous or even well-liked. True dharma is an inner knowing that you are in alignment with something bigger than your fears and needs for external validation.

I have watched hundreds of women express real grief at not knowing their dharma. Whenever I see a woman in a quandary about her life purpose, the first things I ask her are, "What are the moments in your life when you have felt the most joy? And what aspects of your life have brought you the most pain?" In those two remembrances—both the pleasure and the pain—we find signposts toward deeper purpose.

Here are a handful of scenarios I have seen in people I have worked with over the years that may help illustrate how wounds can point us toward our purpose:

The healer who begins his journey by going through a major illness (this is freakishly common and considered a rite of initiation in the shamanic tradition).

The yoga teacher who grew up leaving her body as a young, sensitive girl and needed to re-embody.

The body worker who got interested in anatomy and physiology after an injury.

The activist who grew up being discriminated against.

The interior designer who never had nice things growing up and now creates beautiful homes.

The lawyer who never felt that things were justified or fair in her own family.

The multimillionaire CEO who never felt like he would amount to anything as a boy.

The singer who never felt like she had a voice.

The actress who never felt she was seen.

The amazing father to two young kids who had grown up not knowing his own dad.

The nutritionist who struggled her whole life with body image and an eating disorder.

The writer who writes the book she needs to read. (If you could see me, my hand is raised!)

✳ A GLOW-WORTHY CONTEMPLATION ✳
Challenges into Destiny

Take a moment to consider how your wounds and challenges have been (or may be) the gateway into your purpose. Sometimes the connection may not be as obvious as in the examples above, but quite often we can find a connection between our wounds and the way we show up in service to the world.

This may have been a challenging chapter to read.

But when we work with our pain and are willing to hold space for our wounds, we free up an immense reservoir of untapped energy. Moreover, the things that hold the most pain in our lives have the potential to show us our life's purpose and help us find deeper meaning in our lives. The pain of the wound acts as a crack through which the light of compassion can flow. As we noted earlier, Carl Jung described this ability to hold within us both our wounds and our deeper purpose as "the tension of the opposites"—the paradoxical pull that brings us true wisdom.

Lastly—we do not want to *stay* in our wounds.

We also need to party.

So, skip ahead to the Hell Yes chapter if you need a break from all of this beautiful darkness.

Or read on for the equally beautiful way we can ritualize the act of turning inner wounds into inner glow.

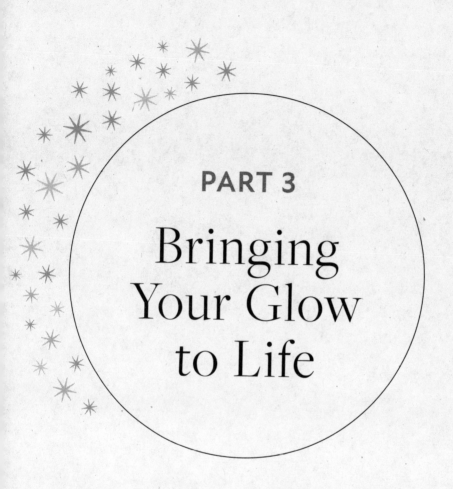

PART 3

Bringing Your Glow to Life

10

Ritual

Without ritual, rite, and ceremony, life can lack a feeling of magic. It is the numinous qualities of life that give us enough light to endure the monotony of our repetitive daily routines. If you feel like your days look like a scene from *The Office*, or you dream of starting your own lady-fight-club just to feel alive, you may be in dire need of more ceremony.

Ceremony helps us step outside our egoistic narratives and limiting perspectives about life. It frees us from isolation by reminding us of our deeper connection with the natural and spiritual worlds and the rich complexity of our own selves—selves that are much bigger than the tiny domain of our mental musings. Without ceremony, our spirits become thirsty for that ineffable glow we've been talking about all throughout this book.

Rituals open us up to the deepest intention of our hearts, making it so much easier to access the part of us that is eternal and unconditional. In addition, rituals remind us that we are not alone. Taking time to honor the elements of the earth, the animals, and our human brothers and sisters helps us remember that there is an "everyone and everything else." Rituals also act as a physical reminder of our own internal complexity.

In other words, rituals and ceremonies are what make life holy. They inject the material world of schedules, work, food preparation, and taking the kids to soccer with intentionality. And we can—I would argue we *must*—bring ceremony into our everyday life if we want to activate the inner radiance we crave.

Recently, I visited a good friend and her husband for a week. I left their house feeling deeply warm inside—a satisfied feeling. Because beyond my love for my friend, there was something else that happened at her house, something holy that we had tapped into. It was a ritual.

Every day, my friend and I would plan our dinner for that night. We would take a pilgrimage to the farmers' market or local store, getting excited about leafy greens, roasted chicken, and mashed potatoes. We would think about her husband and what he might like after a long day on the construction site. We would anticipate the pleasures to come.

As we met in the kitchen to prepare dinner, we would ceremoniously divide the tasks. Amid the aroma of simmering garlic and the sound of potatoes being peeled, we chatted and cracked up over shared memories. It was as if the heat from the bubbling stew on her stove melted away the day's problems and left only warmth behind. Her husband, sweaty and slightly gruff from a day of work, would arrive home and help us set the table—with a real tablecloth, place mats, and napkins! We all turned off our cell phones, sat down together, and looked each other in the eyes.

And then came my favorite part. We lit candles and closed our eyes. I felt the soft palm of my dear friend's hand slip into mine, strongly contrasting with the strong, rough feel of her husband's on my other side. In that circle of our bodies' innocent intimacy, in the glow of the candlelight, we bowed our heads and said grace.

I can't remember the prayer, but I remember the holy, glowing connectedness of that sacred pause. It felt tender. As if, for one moment in our busy day, we could surrender our egos and to-do lists to the reality of our togetherness.

In a very deep way, that loving mealtime ritual made me feel like I had come home and that I was with family.

WHAT IS A RITUAL?

A ritual is an inner or outer action we imbue with a deeper meaning and intention beyond the material realm. All spiritual traditions point us toward some form of ritual. By helping us pause daily life and hold an intention to enter the sacred, rituals encourage us to clarify the mind and remember what matters. Through them, we bring light into our dreary daily routine.

An outer ritual involves the physical world meeting with an inner reality. It can be as simple as pausing during the day to kneel in prayer or bringing our palms together in Namaste before a yoga practice—or as complex as an elaborate traditional ceremony involving physical elements, gestures, movement patterns, songs, and mantras. It is a way of pausing our outer routine in order to shake the mind out of its calcified inner routines.

Inner rituals are more subtle, but equally imbued with intention. Similar to outer rituals, inner rituals of intention, feeling, and visualization allow us to shift the regular pattern of our habitual thoughts, directing them toward both our presence and the sacred. We may imagine an internal bonfire purifying our thoughts. We may visualize our bodies being held within a meaningful symbol. We may also picture breathing in the pain of others on the inhale, and breathing it out, transmuted, on the exhale.

The possibilities—for both inner and outer rituals—are endless. Some rituals are traditional. Others are spontaneous. But what really makes a ritual compelling and transformational is the intention behind it. A sacred ceremony is nothing more or less than an action that *you fill with meaning*. You are what gives your choice of ritual its holiness.

And you don't need a shaman, an incense stick, or a perfected methodology—although they certainly may help! Your ritual can be simple and intuitive. Let's dive into some practical ways that we can use our daily life as an opportunity to remember the holy.

DAILY LIFE AS HOLY RITUAL

Whether we are speaking of prayer, meditation, a movement practice, creative pursuits, mealtime, or even sex (!), bringing simple elements of ceremony to our actions suffuses them with meaning.

Here are some ideas to get your creative juices flowing:

▼ **Wake and sleep with the sacred.** Think of waking as birth and sleeping as death. Before jumping out of bed in the morning, place one hand on your heart and the other on your belly. Take a few moments to feel gratitude for the day, perhaps making an intention to come into the Holy Pause as much as possible. For inspiration in forming evening sleep rituals, think about what we do with little kids. We bathe them, sing to them, rock them, and tell them stories. As adults, we still need these elements of calm and sweetness at nighttime! Move into sleep with a relaxing bath or shower. Place a few drops of lavender on your forehead. Rub your feet with an organic oil and cover them with socks. Take a few minutes to witness your thoughts and feelings about the activity of your day, fully committing to allowing whatever occurred to exist in your mind—the good, bad, and ugly. Practice non-attachment to the day. Think of this as an opportunity to see how much you can surrender your day, your willpower, and your life into the ease of sleep. When thoughts arise, simply come back to the ease of the body, saying the words, "Letting go." This can act as a mental ritual to help you go to sleep with a "digested" mind. For some people, this practice does not always work, as it can stir up more worry. But for others, it can be highly beneficial. Try it, or create your own nighttime ritual to help you rest.

▼ **Feed your pets with love.** Even something as seemingly chore-like as feeding your pets can become a sweet ritual. Use this moment to feel your connection and responsibility to your little creatures, and your appreciation for the joy and comfort they bring to your life.

▼ **Anoint yourself in the bath.** Nurture your glow through self-massage and by anointing your skin with nourishing oils and meaningful symbols. There is no way to do this wrong—simply do what feels great on your skin and muscles. I like to use a warmed organic oil (coconut, jojoba, and almond are a few of my go-tos) and add a few drops of your favorite essential oil. (For more in-depth information on holistic self-care routines, check the resources section.) Sink into a warm tub of water, close your eyes, and soak. Bring your mind into your body, part by part. Imagine placing a small ritual offering inside each of your body parts. Use whatever images feel good to your body. For example, imagine placing a pink rose petal on each eyelid and letting a large drop of honey melt onto your tongue. Use your imagination and intuition. Keep moving through your body parts, waiting for the images to come, until you have filled your whole body with ritual offerings. Consider yourself anointed.

▼ **Embrace the sacred in your journeys.** It's common to offer special prayers in threshold moments of transition across many traditions. One small way you can reconnect to this practice is by saying a little protective prayer or pausing for a moment of reflection before you embark on a trip. You can do the same thing to end a trip, retreat, or special journey with a friend or lover. For example, I recently took my mom on a beach trip. On our last night there, we sat together in the sunset and wrote out the answers to three questions: (1) What were we really grateful for about our time together? (2) What were we willing to leave behind in the winds of the ocean? (3) What were we bringing back with us into our lives? Before we left on our separate flights the next morning, we read our answers to each other. It was simple, real, and special.

▼ **Connect your meditation to a sense of holiness.** Meditate, if possible, in the same place daily to imbue that area with a quality of the numinous. Before you begin, clear the space and set your intentions by burning sage or lighting your favorite incense or candle and offering a mantra or prayer out loud. Something as simple as, "May my practice be for the benefit of all beings" can transform the practice from a solitary act into an act of service.

▼ **Research your lineage's traditions.** Learning and reconnecting with the origins of common holidays can be extremely fulfilling. For example, Christmas is an opportunity to remember that many of our ancestors celebrated the winter solstice as a time of both the dying of the solar light and the rising of the sun in the spring. It was a time for lighting candles and surrounding the home with lights, small gifts, and family gatherings as a celebration of *the hope that comes through death*. The Christian tradition borrowed from more Earth-based pagan traditions that understood the birth, death, and resurrection of the sun (or son). For me, it is truly satisfying to connect the Christianity of my youth to the nature-goddess lover inside. Try researching your own favorite holidays and traditions; you can then develop and share meaningful rituals with your family and friends that instill these times with sacred intention.

THE RITUAL OF MEALTIME

Eating food is a ritual all humans share, and it is such a fertile ground for ritual that it deserves its own list. If you are like me, it is all too easy to rush through mealtimes, shoveling food in your mouth unaware or—even worse—zoning out in front of the TV. Many spiritual traditions invite us to use mealtime as a moment to practice understanding how interconnected we are with the earth. When we consider all the elements that went into the meal on our plate, we see the rain, sun, and wind . . . the farmers' hands, the dense soil, the earthworms . . . and on and on it goes. Total interrelatedness.

Here are a few methods that help imbue meals with ritual:

▼ Hide your phone and turn off your computer. Create a tech-free space that will allow your taste buds to be present to the pleasure of food.

▼ Eat somewhere pleasant when possible. Nature is ideal—look out a window if you are stuck inside, or at the very least buy a little potted plant to accompany you as you eat.

▼ Make your environment special. Even when you are alone, you can always light a candle and/or lay down a place mat.

▼ Before you begin eating, try taking three breaths to relax the body and awaken the "rest and digest" parasympathetic nervous system.

▼ Say a prayer of gratitude for the food.

▼ Eat with awareness of the food, contemplating the complex web of interconnection that brought it to your plate, chewing slowly and savoring each mouthful before taking the next.

▼ Try to eat at the same time daily. This helps condition the body and the mind for optimal digestion and presence.

▼ Don't eat when angry or upset. It's better to pause and feel those emotions when you experience them, then wait to eat until you feel hungry.

Elemental Rituals with Mer Hogan

One of my favorite ways to add ritual to my life involves working with and in the natural world. Here, my best friend, colleague, and shamanic ceremonial guide Mer Hogan suggests a few of her favorite ritual offerings to bring the elements into our ceremonial life.

Working with the Elements

Earth: The earth is the common ground upon which we all stand. She is a mother, teacher, healer, composter, provider, and giver of all that we enjoy and revere about our existence. To practice honoring the earth ritually, spend time communing with the earth and its plants (see "Plant Listening" below). If you have a garden, tend to it lovingly, and connect to the plants with all your senses. If you compost, ask the earth to help you turn both your physical and mental rubbish into fertile soil. Or simply stand outside in your bare feet, feeling the calm, loving presence of the earth while you send love down and pull love up. Lie on your belly in the grass and speak or sing your thanks into her heart. Weep your pain into her as well.

Alternatively, you can rock out! Find a stone that calls to you, and ask it to be your ally. Let this stone friend help you move anxiety, worry, and loneliness out of your cells. Sit with the stone and the feeling you want to honor and shift. Take a deep breath as you feel the feeling, then blow it into the stone. Do this over and over until you feel your energy settle. Thank the stone, then lay it back down onto Mother Earth. If you'd like, you can even create a special place in your yard for a rock garden of prayers.

Water: Water is the dominant element in the body, and it seems to be highly responsive to our intentions, emotion, and energy. Ritualizing with water can be as simple as saying a blessing on your drinking water. Give the water a little swirl inside your glass, then drink it deeply into your cells.

To work further with water blessings, set a crystal or glass bowl outside the next time it rains. Collect the sky's water and bless it in your own way—for example, you might add crystals or flowers to the bowl. Blow your prayers and gratitude into the bowl before letting them soak. Later, take the bowl to your local creek, river, or shore, and allow your blessed water to rejoin the eternal water cycle of our planet.

Air: Breath is life. It is the great pulse of existence and the winds of our body. We inhale the exhalation of the trees, and they inhale ours. We are being breathed together. We can change our entire state by changing the way we draw in, contain, and release this light-swirling element of air. To honor air, inhale slowly and deeply, thinking of breath as spiritual nectar. Exhale with gratitude for this opportunity to be alive.

Remember, your voice is also breath. Make a commitment to embody beauty and truth through your voice. Choose your words carefully and listen carefully as well. Deep listening is one of the most sacred forms of communication, which is an everyday expression of the air element.

But our breathing is not the only means to commune with air! The next time you feel the winds kick up, go out and dance with them. When your dance is done, be still and listen to the wind with your whole body. Its wild force brings the blessings of change and can reveal great wisdom.

Fire: Fire is dynamic, and oh so alive. Since the moment humans discovered how to make and tend fire, we have gathered around it to share songs, stories, and wisdom. Fire is our ritual center, the natural reminder of our glowing inner light. This may be one reason why we love sitting around it! To awaken fire ritually, go outdoors and face the east as the sun is on the rise, and thank it for its life-giving radiance. Draw the light into your hands and pass it over your body. Ask the energy of the sun to activate the balanced fire energy within your cells and your consciousness. In the evening, face the west and give blessings and gratitude to the sun for this day that you had to be alive and to learn. Out loud, tell the setting sun three things you loved about the day, and blow the sun a kiss goodnight.

Plant Listening

It is important to connect with nature both within and beyond the four elements. Plants are an ideal place to start! They are fantastic guides and helpers, and humans have been learning from them for a long time. Go outside and take a quiet moment to be with nature. Look around, and when you see a plant you feel drawn to, relax your body and ask the plant if you may come and visit. Feel for a clear "yes" or "no" (this may come as a feeling of being welcomed or a feeling that you should move on). Trust whatever information you get—the biggest way we sabotage our inner knowing is doubt.

Once you have been welcomed, observe the plant with all your senses and thank it for the qualities you observe. For example, maybe you notice the softness and roundness of the plant's leaves, its fragrance and color, the strength of its stem, or the way it sways in the breeze. Maybe you receive the message that just like the leaves, you too can soften and sway, trusting the strength of your center. Once you've fully connected to the plant, thank it for the visit and the message, and leave a small stone, flower, or other small offering as a gift.

Candle Fire Blessing

A Candle Fire Blessing is a wonderful ritual for the new or full moon. Here's how to do it:

- ▼ Bring your hands to your heart.
- ▼ Create a sacred container around you where you can be quiet. This might mean closing doors, asking your partner to keep the kids, or shutting down all technological devices.
- ▼ Light a candle and gaze into the flame. As you watch it dance, bring your hands close to the flame and take in its light and heat.
- ▼ Feed the warmth and heat to your belly and bless your ability to walk the walk of your life in integrity.
- ▼ Do the same with the light. Feed it to your heart. Feel the fire's light relax your chest and bless yourself with the gift of a harmonious relationship. Say, "May I be in harmony internally and in my relationships. Show me the way to love."
- ▼ Once more, gather up the light of the fire. Bring it to your third eye and into your brain. Say, "Show me how to see opportunity in life's moments and challenges. Awaken my spiritual sight so I can see and be a force for beauty."
- ▼ Thank the fire. Blow out the flame and close with a gesture of gratitude such as bringing your hands to your heart or bowing.

ANCESTRAL OFFERINGS

One of the most powerful uses of ritual lies in honoring where we come from: our biological ancestors, as well as our cultural and spiritual roots. Though many of us have lost these practices, working with ancestors through ceremony has long been a part of cultures throughout the world. Honoring your lineage through an intentional ritual can be a very intimate, tender, and beautiful way to clear the pain from your past, while respecting where you come from. Whether you feel connected with your ancestral traditions and ceremonial practices or feel orphaned from them, you can work intuitively to craft sacred rituals that strike a chord of connection between you and the Divine.

I want to begin this section in the way of all of our ancestors—and tell a story of my people.

Amongst a collection of family photos on a table in my home sits a picture of my great-granddaddy Jesse. He's in the mountains of Copper Creek, Virginia, crossing a rickety old bridge he's walked over a hundred times. Holding a cane and wearing a soft old jacket, my ancestor looks down at the precarious wooden bridge. I imagine him carefully, slowly placing his worn-out feet one in front of the other. Slowly because he is old, or perhaps because back then there was nothing much to hurry about.

Every time I see that photo of my great-grandfather, I am filled with pride. He lived to be a hundred years old. Legend holds that he was a good man who took care of his kin and neighbors and would meet the sundown by reading his Bible and taking a little shot of whiskey.

My mama tells me the same stories of him over and over. She tells me how my grandfather, Wild Bill, would wash those same feet in the photo at the end of my great-grandfather's days. I wonder if she knows how many times she's told me those stories. But it doesn't really matter. Because the stories are so few, they are precious. And in the telling of them, we feel connected to our ancestors in an intangible and powerful way that opens a door from us, the living, to them, the dead.

If the men in my ancestral line walked the mountains and drank whiskey, the women carried the lineage of great beauty and kindness—and a love of peanut butter and honey. I can still see my grandma Mary Belle standing in her tiny 1950s galley kitchen late at night, bingeing on its sweetness and fat. She waits for my granddaddy to come home from the bowling alley he owned. But she knows good and well he'll be late. And when he arrives, he will smell of that same whiskey that rocked his father to bed each night. Mary Belle's honey-jar-lovin' blood passed right along to my mama, Vera Loraine, and then down into me.

Within our genealogy, we hold echoes of the behavior patterns of those who came before us. We hold their pain, struggles, abuses, and addictions, as well as their gifts and talents. Our ancestors live within us as traces of memories. Our bodies remember the babies lost in childbirth, the husbands who never came home from war, and the grief of leaving our ancestral homes or being robbed of them. Within us, our body knows in a way the mind does not.

A GLOW-WORTHY CONTEMPLATION
Ancestral Return

Consider your grandparents, great-grandparents, and even beyond. Do you know what they ate? What kind of air they breathed? Was it a seaside wetness? The humidity of the forest? A drying desert wind? What climate did they walk in? Was it sultry heat or bracing cold? What challenges did they face? Heartbreaks? Traumas? What triumphs did they have? What obstacles were they able to overcome?

Religions from around the globe have long venerated the spirits of our ancestors and the role that they play in our lives. So much of our collective dysphoria and anxiety comes from the fact that many of us have lost access to these practices and feel no connection with our ancestral roots. Fortunately, more and more people who have lost this spiritual tradition are beginning to rediscover it.

Even modern science is coming around, with research showing that our bodies store our ancestors' emotional legacies. From our DNA and epigenetic regulation of gene expression to our everyday emotional experience, our ancestors influence our personalities and preferences. So many of our anxieties, addictions, chronic diseases, and unexplained emotional tendencies likely originate not from our individual life experiences or a chemical imbalance in our brains, but instead with our ancestors.

Honoring our lineages and working through their pain has the capacity to rewire our brains and bodies, freeing our DNA from karmic tendencies we hold from our ancestors. On a spiritual level, this process also helps us open a channel to receive the love and support of the ancestral realm. Ceremonially working with our ancestors lets us move out of painful patterns as they begin to emerge.

I have often seen the beneficial effects of working with ancestral ceremonies. These rituals help us process and integrate ancient family traumas, secrets, and addictions, freeing us from the grips of our lineage's afflictions and compulsions. Ancestral ceremonies can also restore a sense of personal connection to the sacred as we realize we are not atomized entities, separated from our historical lines, but torch carriers of their unfulfilled legacies.

Often, working to remember our ancestors also helps us kindle compassion and forgiveness for them. We gain a deep understanding of what they went through as children and adults, and even in their worst times, we begin to see that they were doing the best they could given their life situation and state of mind. As we offer our ancestors greater love and forgiveness, we also liberate ourselves from lineage-based pain pathways that run through our being. And as we bear witness to both the pain our people went through and their gifts, we can choose to bolster the positive and transmute the pain into strength. This work can help free us from old emotions, as well as from energetic and even physical issues we may not even know we're carrying.

CREATING AN ANCESTRAL RITUAL

As a first step in connecting to your ancestors as a link to the unseen world, I suggest researching the traditions of your own people.

Does your family have a tradition of working with those who have passed on? If not, don't worry! We will walk through some general guidelines for ceremony work as well as a simple ancestral ritual. It is important not to get caught up in getting the outer ritual perfect—all you need is to connect to an authentic feeling in your heart. As you begin your ancestor work, remember that your faith and willingness are way more important than getting every step just right.

Ancestor Work Basics: The Importance of Compassion

Generally speaking, ancestor ritual is based around three core premises:

1. Differentiation brings truth and understanding.
2. Truth and understanding bring compassion.
3. Compassion heals.

Let's break these down. First, in order to honor and truly see our ancestors, we must separate ourselves from them and their past experiences. This is why ancestral rituals often involve setting up photos of the ancestors and offering them gifts. This gives them a seat at the table while also allowing us to see our own selves as separate from them. Through this separation, we see their lives more clearly. We can also rest in knowing that we are not the things that happened to our ancestors, although we may be called to witness and even feel those things in the present.

The more clearly we can see our ancestors' lives, the more we can feel compassion—the most healing, holy force on the planet. As you begin to work with your lineage, start from a place of deep faith in the power of compassion to heal the terrible things that may be brought to the surface when you explore the past. Think of yourself as the result of your lineage. In addition to feeling what your ancestors felt, you also have the opportunity to see what was unseen and hear what was unheard in the past. Through your intention you can be a vessel for what is undigested in your lineage, but you are also your own person, able to free yourself from the negative past experiences of the ancestral realm.

As you practice, try not to get caught up in the stories or emotions that arise through your ancestral lines. Simply let emotions, memories, and images move through you, and embrace them all as a compassionate witness.

Crafting a Simple Ancestral Ceremony

Here are my ritual-expert friend Meredith Hogan's guidelines for performing a simple ancestral ceremony:

▼ First, make sure you act in faith. You've gotta trust that the rituals work! They wouldn't have survived over thousands of years and existed all over the world if they weren't effective.

▼ Humbly ask for auspicious support and Divine guidance. Begin by allowing the Divine to lead you toward the ancestral connections within you that are most in need of healing. At first, you may want to work with someone who is emotionally close to you, but the ancestors who need to come through and be honored are not always the ones you have the strongest bonds with.

▼ Welcome whomever you find. Be with each ancestor in gratitude and reverence. Listen to and trust the experiences that come.

▼ Ask your ancestor why they have come forward. What needs to be honored? What was their greatest passion? Their greatest challenge? Their deepest regret? Did they have a dream? Was it fulfilled? If not, what got in their way? Try not to emotionally indulge or repress. Make a sincere effort to remain unattached and differentiated from whatever emotions you feel or whatever images you see as you work with each ancestor.

▼ If you find it helpful, write down what you receive from them. Then, ask them if they have a gift or any words of wisdom to share with you.

▼ There will come a time when the experience feels complete. Thank your ancestor for coming. See them outside of you. In front of you. And eventually taking their leave. As the ritual concludes, bow to the ancestral realm, giving final thanks.

Creating an Ancestral Altar

An altar is a material expression of sacred remembrances, both personal and collective. If you would like to anchor your ancestral practice in the physical world, you can create your own ancestral altar. It can be easy and intuitive, creative and fulfilling. Remember, the altar is not decorative or simply a collection of memorabilia; it is a functional portal through which we work to heal our bloodlines. The altar is a living energy vortex, and diving into it can cause our prayers to be answered, our bodies healed, and our spiritual lives emboldened.

Here are some easy steps to get you started in creating your own home altar:

1. Decide where your altar will live. Choose a place in your home that is relatively low in traffic. If it can be hidden from view, even better. Do not place your altar in a bedroom or bathroom, as energy flow in these places is oppositional to what is needed for a grounded, ancestral space.

2. Choose a table or other surface for your altar.

3. Place framed photos and/or the ashes of your ancestors on the altar, if available. If not, use objects that may represent your ancestors, such as a favorite piece of jewelry, a pocket knife, or a scarf.

4. Add food and offerings that your ancestors would like. Things like sweets, milk, fruits, honey, and other tasty substances are common in traditional rituals the world over. I have seen rum, banana pudding, chilaquiles, whiskey, and even a smoking pipe and cigarettes used in ancestor rituals. Remember to replace the food as needed.

5. Incorporate your lineage's traditions. The shrine should hold sacred objects that your ancestors would connect to, irrespective of your current religious beliefs. For example, my ancestors were Christian, so I have a Bible on my altar out of respect for their prayers and practices. Bring whatever objects compel you to experience the sacred within your ancestry. One of my first spiritual teachers, A. G. Mohan, instructed me to pray in the words of my ancestors because they would be more responsive to hymns, prayers, and verses that aligned with their beliefs. This does not mean you need to use only these objects and words, but it can help when specifically working with your lineage.

6. Add light. Traditionally, altars have some form of candle, lamp, or other flame. I typically use candles.

7. Bring in the elements. For example, you may include incense for air, a candle for fire, water for water, and a crystal or rock for earth. However, you can use other elements (or representations) as well. I usually add a feather for space.

8. Include your own *personal* connection to Divinity. Add an object to the altar that represents this connection. For my altar, I've brought in

statues of Jesus, Mary, Quan Yin, and the Buddha. I have seen altars with Kali, Mother Nature, the archangel Michael, or photos of gurus who now guide the student as ancestors. Objects like these help you connect with a deeper matrix of spiritual support.

9. Pray to your ancestors as guides. Work with ancestors who feel supportive and loving to you. Ask your wise ancestors to show up and be with you. Some ancestors may bring a lot of pain and suffering. As we discussed before, we can love and differentiate ourselves from those ancestors. Allow yourself to be a compassionate witness to their pain, while also feeling yourself as a separate being, whole and complete unto yourself.

Getting Support around Ancestral Trauma

For many who are new to the concept of ancestor rituals, the idea of working with the dead can be unnerving. And that's okay! As with all the techniques in this book, work with this practice only if you feel called to and ready for it. It is also important to understand that working with ancestral content can bring up traumatic material. If this is true for you, it can be helpful to find a guide to work with you through painful ancestral content (especially where there is a feeling of overwhelm).

RITUALS OF AMAZING GRACE

Let me close this chapter by telling you about one of the most beautiful ancestor rituals I have ever experienced. It happened deep in the woods of Virginia, where I was invited to initiate a full moon ritual for a private festival hosted by a large group of friends.

Now, I'm used to teaching courses and practices to tattooed yoga girls in flowy dresses as much as stay-at-home moms in stretch pants. That day, standing on the banks of a river, I was suddenly surrounded by not only women, but also their bearded, flannel-wearing, beer-drinking mountain men.

Over the next two hours, the guys really surprised me. They showed up completely. They gave themselves to the breathwork, meditation, and depth inquiries, despite these being new experiences for many of them, and certainly not ones that society taught or encouraged for them.

It was a powerful spiritual awakening for me to be with these men. Sitting around a bonfire, I watched all my preconceived notions of "how men are" (they don't do rituals) and "what a sacred ceremony should be like" (beer cans are taboo) burn up as I witnessed these men deeply feel, intuit, and articulate their inner lives.

Toward the end of the ritual, gathered in a circle surrounded by flowers, candles, fruits, incense, and offerings, I asked them to remember an ancestor and let that ancestor come to them (much like Mer asked you to do earlier in this chapter). Afterwards, I opened up the space to share our experiences. We sat quietly, listening to the babbling song of the river and the chirping of late summer cicadas. I was worried no one would share. But then one of the men, a stoic, quiet type, finally broke the silence.

"I saw my granddad," he said softly, tears welling up in the corners of his wrinkled eyes.

"He was sittin' on the porch singin' to me, like he used to do when I was a kid. I mean, it was wild. I could really hear him . . . and he was singin' and tellin' me it was all gonna be alright."

And with that, that big, gruff Virginian man began to sing the words that so many of our ancestors once sang.

Amazing grace
How sweet the sound
That saved a wretch like me.
I once was lost, but now I'm found
Was blind, but now I see.

Needless to say, there wasn't a dry eye present. His ancestor had shown up, and it clearly had a healing effect on him. But perhaps more importantly, *his own willingness to feel had been healing for all of us.* His tears were our medicine.

As we reconnect with our ancestors, amazing grace can begin to flow. Grace is a force of effortless universal compassion and forgiveness. Through this force, we see who we really are behind the habits, hang-ups, addictions, and traumas of our ancestors, but also—perhaps more importantly—we realize that their wisdom and love are also guiding us. We are no longer alone in the endeavor to be free. Grace is both deeply personal and also collective. It can feel like an unexpected, and often undeserved, blessing. Grace is surprising because the ego cannot create it. It is magic precisely because it breaks with the conscious mind's expected outcomes.

We are the culmination of everything our ancestors worked so hard for. As you read these words, pause a moment to *feel* within yourself the lineage that produced you. You are their eyes that see, their mouth that can voice their unspoken longings. You are their hands, and you can act for them now. You are their feet and legs, and you can walk toward goodness—and away from what isn't right anymore. You are their heart. It is a great honor to be here now, capable of feeling and releasing what they had to hide. They are here with you, rooting you on. They want you to step into your best self and highest evolution. What you do is not just for you, but your whole people. They want you to glow. And they know you are deeply worthy of the task.

And in the end, we perform our rituals for the benefit of all humans.

We are, after all, one big family.

Sex

If you want to know how truly glow-worthy you feel, sex is a direct mirror. It's as if the most intimate realm of our being were God's mischievous magnifying glass, supercharging our deepest longings and bringing that which we are most terrified of into stark relief. Sex awakens the dormant energy within, bringing to the surface our most ancient vulnerabilities as well as our holy potentialities of creation and destruction. This primal energy can, when used mindfully, awaken a fierce inner fire that enlivens our vitality and melts away our old patterns and habits. When used unconsciously, it can inflict pain and deepen our embeddedness (pardon the pun) in our oldest personal and ancestral karma.

This chapter will walk you through some ways of relating to the power and holiness of your sexual self. It will also offer some techniques for releasing the old belief systems about sex that you may have picked up along the way. In this sense, we can purify the primal creative force of our bodies. Not purify as in "ooh, you are dirty and bad," but purify as in you can experience more of what you *really* want by coming from a place of fullness rather than lack, informed by the deepest loving desire of your heart.

Purifying your sexual self means that your true sexual sovereignty can emerge. In other words, you can access inner wisdom in your sexual expressions. Your choices can come from love, whether you choose to be sexually celibate or a polyamorous sex-worker dominatrix!

Sex energy. We all have it, no matter who we are or who we're dating or having sex with or whether we're having sex at all (or even want to have sex at all!). Sex energy is sex energy, irrespective of your biological sex, what your body looks like, your gender, who you are attracted to, or what you identify as. Biology and our hormones certainly play a role in our sexual experience, but, as we have learned in this book, we aren't solely biological creatures—we are energetic, emotional, soulful creations. Many ancient mystical belief systems understood that gender is never as simple as biology—and we are all multi-gendered on an energetic and spiritual level, each of us possessing both the yin/feminine and yang/masculine capacities. It is my hope that regardless of your sex or gender, you can embrace the holiness of however your sexuality expresses itself.

So, with that, let's dive deeper into all things soul, spirit, and S-E-X.

DOUGHNUTS AND CHASTITY PROMISE CARDS

There is nothing like growing up in a Southern Baptist church for ending up with some pretty guilty feelings around your sexual "worldly" self.

I can almost see myself there again: I'm sixteen years old, full of libidinal charge, and hoping a cute boy named Luke will notice me. I'm at a church lock-in, where I will be sealed into an annex overnight with a hundred other pimple-ridden, awkward teens. We are packed into the church pews like sardines, fed all-you-can-eat Krispy Kreme doughnuts, and made to endure low-budget education flicks about the everlasting hellfire that results from one dreaded sin: Sex Before Marriage.

High on sugar, sleep deprivation, and the theatrical swells of contemporary Christian emo-rock, I was surprised to see even the most hardened of my teenage friends raise his hand when asked if he wanted to "be saved." My heart softened, watching these people commit themselves to Jesus. Those of us who were already saved could get "recommitted to Christ."

Over the years in the church, I was "recommitted" countless times, oscillating constantly between giving my life to Jesus and hoping my latest crush would notice me. That weekend of the lock-in, I signed a sex promise-card, assuring God that I would never "give my sexual self away" before I was a bride dressed in white.

You can probably guess how well that went. For college, I moved to Europe, and as many a young Baptist, Mormon, Catholic, or Muslim girl has done, I went "wild," drinking vodka and swinging from the chandeliers at seven-story Spanish discotecas, delighting in make-out sessions with men who couldn't pronounce my name.

Thank God, that wild young woman eventually found other perspectives (and great mentors). They helped me reformat my understanding of my sexual nature and my sexual sovereignty.

Trust Yourself

If this part of the book is making you cringe, just know this: *Ancient teachings are unavoidably conservative.* They are "that which was conserved and preserved." That's because a lot of them are really wise. But some of them need an update. What that means is that you, dear reader, get to learn to find and trust your own intuition. I encourage you to let these more old-school possibilities sit with you. What works, use. What you can't stand, let go. It may come back to you with time.

What I learned from over twenty years of deep study into ancient wisdom (including Tantra) was that *sex energy is prana*—life force. And that within the realm of our body's sacred energy, there are no rules. Nothing is specifically good or bad, just energy moving us toward or away from our heart's real longing.

The ancients saw sexual energy as a force that could be channeled into our *satya kama* or *asatya kama*. Your satya kama is the pulsation of your sexuality that leads you to more love and true fulfillment. It is the vibrancy of sexuality *alchemized* within you. It is co-creation with the Divine that enables you to get what your heart *really* wants (underneath all the confusion and subconscious stuff). Your asatya kama is the pulsation of your sexuality that brings you more misery and (unhelpful) karma, and usually takes the form of you repeating the painful relational dynamics of your family history. I mean, how many of us have gotten into relationships that were more "wound-mate" than "soulmate"?

By this point, you have already learned a key takeaway: *You are the only one who can discern the truth of what your heart really wants.* From the perspective of karma, you are the only one who can discern, through deep inquiry within, whether your sexual energy is heading toward love and true fulfillment or misery.

Okay, so how do we start to heal and bring more holiness into our sexual life so we can truly get what our heart wants? How can our sex life start to become less weird and painful and more full of light?

A good place to start is to consider the idea that our spiritual life *must include and honor* our sexual desire. This doesn't mean we should just run out and start hooking up with everyone we feel attracted to. It might actually mean taking a sex break to be able to hear the voice of our heart's deepest longing and purify our asatya kama. It could also mean that if we are partnered, we start listening to the inner voice that says, "I know my sex life could be more fulfilling. I want more."

YOU ARE A KAMA YONI

"Kama (desire) was born first. Neither gods nor ancestors nor
men can equal him. Oh! You are immense as you reside in
all living things. I bow before you . . . You are a higher deity
than the sun, moon, wind, and fire . . . You are assimilated
in all and therefore you are forever great. I bow to you."
—Atharva Veda

The ancient teachings say that all of us are *kama yonis,* or "wombs of desire." Kama doesn't just mean hedonic sexual pleasure. It also means sensuality, the enjoyment of life, and even bodily ease. (Sexual intercourse is just one among millions of sensual experiences we can have!) And so, here we are, constantly birthing new desires and predestined to want pleasure. I mean, God wanted you, so it makes sense that you also want things. And all of that is okay. The trick here is to have your body's sexual longings be filled with spiritual glow.

You see, for many ancient cultures, sex was seen as a healthy part of daily life. It was accepted, instead of compartmentalized as it is today. It was not excessive and shameful. Sexual relationships were seen as nested within the greater context of society. Sex was held within the cultural frame of the sacred. Ayurvedic medicine and Tantra understood the ways in which individual sexual health was reflected in the health of the greater society, and vice versa. Priestesses, prophets, and physicians were awake to the healing force of sexual energy. Imagine this: You go to the doc about a belly ache or a bout of depression, and in addition to inquiring about your physical body, your physician asks you about you how fulfilling your sex life is!

"Great," you may be thinking. "So, what should I do, just study the *Kama Sutra*?"

Well, you could. But that book was written by men for men and during a particularly patriarchal period in India two thousand years ago. And don't get me wrong, there are some good things about the *Kama Sutra*. It can, for example, help us remove shame from our sexuality. But as with many other ancient teachings, *women's practices either were not recorded, were burned, or were systemically devalued*. I have included a few of the rare women's sex manuals from ancient times in the resources section of this book. Based on my research, they are few and far between.

For this reason, we have to rely on multiple sources of information, as well as the greatest source of all: *our own bodies and our intuition*. Our greatest chance for sexual empowerment and sexual sovereignty lies in that Holy Pause that we have discussed throughout the book.

BALANCING YOUR HUSTLE

Sexual health arises naturally when we have a healthy balance between our yin and yang aspects. That means owning the part of you that wants to fulfill a heroic mission, launch your ambitions into the world, and be a lady boss. It also means equally valuing the part of you that needs to take a break, have a really great orgasm, drink a juice, and let someone else serve you.

Our society embeds in women the false, unhealthy idea that we have value only when we are sweet and nurturing, making nice food and plump babies. Similarly, society also pushes the false belief that we have value only if we are achieving awards, making cash, or hustling on some kind of "grind." Sexual holiness (and hormonal balance) requires balancing these two polarities, but also requires that we go beyond them, spiritualizing our life and our needs through our intuition and practices, like the ones outlined in this book.

✱✱ A GLOW-WORTHY RECIPE ✱✱
Ojas Sex Shake

Ancient Ayurveda understood our sexual robustness to be deeply tied to our overall immunity and resiliency. They called this force *ojas*. This is a great smoothie you can make to get your libido on point. It is also a great post-orgasmic tonic for men, who deplete much of their vital reserve through orgasm. As with any herbal advice, always consult with a health-care practitioner, especially if you are pregnant, breastfeeding, or taking pharmaceutical drugs. Note that I get my herbs from Banyan Botanicals.

Ingredients

- ▼ 10 skinless almonds
- ▼ 5 dates, pitted
- ▼ 2 cups milk (any kind)
- ▼ ½ teaspoon ashwagandha
- ▼ ½ teaspoon kapikacchu
- ▼ ½ teaspoon vidari kanda
- ▼ ½ teaspoon maca
- ▼ ¼ teaspoon ground cinnamon (You can also the add same amount of ground cardamom, fennel, and/or ginger.)
- ▼ Pinch of ground nutmeg

Preparation

1. If you wish, soak the almonds and dates overnight, then drain. (This makes them more digestible, but it isn't required.)
2. In a small saucepan, bring the milk to a low boil. Add the herbs and spices and whisk.
3. Pour the milk mixture into a blender, add the almonds and dates, and blend on high for 30 to 60 seconds, until completely smooth.

YOUR BED IS AS IMPORTANT AS YOUR THRONE

Yes, you are a queen—instrumental in your own life, and in the lives of others. And it can be fun to feel like a boss-bitch royal leader who can hone and craft a life she loves. A well-checked to-do list turns me on as much as the next woman. But if we live only in our instrumental, get-it-done selves, we are misshapen, forgetting that a queen not only needs a throne—she also needs a bed.

What do I mean by bed?

In a literal sense, I mean sleep and rest. Buy the best bed you can afford. You spend a third of your life there (if you are lucky). Invest in good nighttime routines. Make sleep a big fat priority in your life, and I assure you, your queendom will prosper.

But a bed also metaphorically represents being at ease and resting in who we already are—not needing to become something or someone else. In bed, we don't have to do much in order to prove our value. The bed is all about being present and receptive. It is opening to the grace, love, and abundance *that is already here.*

Need more bed, less throne? What follows is a breath practice that helps awaken the parasympathetic, life-is-easy, receptive nervous system. This breath has been shown in research studies to help calm the nervous system, tone the vagus nerve, and lower blood pressure, and has been used in the treatment of chronic pain, anxiety, PTSD, insomnia, and depression.

A GLOW-WORTHY MEDITATION

The Most Relaxing Breath Ever

Find a comfortable seat or lie down. Breathe in through your nose, easily and naturally, for a count of four. Feel a gentle expansion outward in your diaphragm (that is, out to the sides more than up toward your head). Pause for a count of four. The pause should be effortless. If it is not, simply reduce the length of the pause. Then breathe out through your nose in the same slow, smooth way for a count of four. Pause the breath at the bottom of the exhale for another count of four. In the pauses, cultivate a deep sense of openness, rest, and receptivity.

GLOW-WORTHY IS SEX-WORTHY

A core part of living a truly integrated (aka glow-filled) life is the radical acceptance that you are a sexual creature. We need sexual energy and immunity to supercharge our spiritual journey. Many of the ancient teachings revolve around staying "juicy"—receptive to nurturance—and hormonally healthy as both a prerequisite and an outcome of living an authentic spiritual life. The sex force feeds the spiritual force. And the spiritual force rejuvenates our hearts, emotions, minds, and bodies, letting us retain our youthful enthusiasm and libido regardless of the number of years we have lived.

A GLOW-WORTHY CONTEMPLATION

The Inner Queendom Check-in

Let's take a moment to check in with our inner queendom. Here are some inquiries that may spark your awakening into the part of you that longs for both a bed and a throne. Remember, it is in our honesty around these inquiries that we bring more light to our sexuality and awaken the inner glow of our true worth.

*How turned on are you by both your intimate partner
(if you have one) and your life in general?*

Do you wake up rested and excited (turned on!) by what you get to do today?

*How much do you feel like you are sucking the
juice out of this one, precious life?*

*How much are you running on fumes? Exhausted? In charge
but secretly longing for someone else to take over?*

*What is the state of your sleep, immunity, and overall
health? How easily are you able to resist both physical and
psychic pathogens? (Emotional vampires, anyone?)*

*What is your relationship to pleasure? Are you able to give yourself
the room and permission to receive the experience of pleasure? Do you
savor life or rush through to get to the next task? Do you have moments
throughout the day when you feel your body's pleasurable aliveness?*

*Are you able to drop into the parasympathetic nervous system? (This is the
rest/digest aspect of our being. I think of it as feeling healthy, happy, and horny.)*

What is your relationship to play? What do you do for fun?

*How much permission have you given to yourself to want
things? Examples include sex, authentic connection,
nourishing food, safety, and even ecstatic experiences.*

*How capable are you, right now, of resting in your open-hearted,
receptive self (the one who needs nothing to be whole and complete)?*

HONORING THE HOLINESS OF YOUR
INNER SEX GODDESSES

Another way to bring more holiness to your sexual life is to think of your sexuality as holding three goddesses. You may relate to one or more of them as more
"acceptable." You may find others more taboo. All of them need a sacred frame.

One is the sex jaguar. She is the part of you that is a wild animal. She can smell her partner's T-shirt and go sex-crazy. She wants to bite, scratch, and be dominated or dominate. Straight up, she is the part of you that wants to be ravished, and we need to let her be acknowledged! If not, she will get rageful when her partner doesn't know to throw her down and absolutely ravage her. She is primal sex incarnate.

Another is the rose-covered mama. She is the part of you that is creative and life-giving. There is a giving, nurturing sweetness in her sexuality (whether she uses that sweetness and receptivity for making a baby or making love). She wants to make love slowly, covered in rose petals, and surrounded by candlelight, in a way that is dedicated to sensuality. She is filled with emotion and wants a heart connection. She is romance incarnate.

The last is the light bringer. She is the part of you that is pure spirit and pure wisdom. She knows that sex can lead her to the Divine. She is the enduring wisdom of a fully awakened sexuality. As she makes love, she sees herself and her partner as both transcendent and temporary. She uses sex to purify. She brings forth that which is taboo and hidden and heals it through love. She sees the god inside her lover and inside herself. She is the part of you that can witness both your sexual emotion and sweetness and the primal sex jaguar within—both inner Madonna and inner whore—but transcends all duality. She is sexual holiness incarnate.

It's important to give room to each of these sex goddesses. Feel free to give them names of your own, or even make up a few new ones! The point is that we give time and acceptance to each aspect of our sexuality, giving each of them a sacred place at the table, rather than trying to be *only* one.

YOUR SEX WAVES

Another way to bring a sacred perspective to your sexual life is to understand your stages of sexual arousal. According to Ayurveda, you have three. The first stage is *tamas,* or dullness (the inner sex-tigress is asleep). The second stage is *rajas,* or passion (the inner sex-tigress is awake and ready to play/pounce). The third stage is *sattva,* or contentment and clarity (the inner sex-tigress is at rest, satisfied, and basking in the sex-glow that brings wisdom and health).

Tamas: Sleeping Tigress Mode

In the tamas phase, we are just not turned on. And that's a good thing. We don't want to walk around having orgasms all day. In this stage, our sexuality is asleep. And so, if we want to tap into our dormant sexual energy, we need to do something to wake it up. For some people, and at some points in our life and relationships, it's easy to wake the sleeping tigress. But for many of us, we sometimes need some help.

For some of you reading this book, your libido has dried up so much that it's not as easy as just nudging the sleeping sex-cat. It's more complicated.

You see, over my many years of working with thousands of women, I have seen a disturbing pattern that is a massive libido destroyer: *the false belief that my marriage/relationship/sex life has gone south. It is all my fault. And it's my job to fix it.*

Here is the thing: Your body doesn't lie. Your sex life is a direct mirror of your true, often subconscious feelings about yourself, your body, your relationship, and your life. Ayurveda says that one of the main reasons a woman's libido disappears is stress. A woman who is giving out more than she is taking in, or serving more than she is receiving, will see that reflected in her sexuality. Another reason a woman's libido disappears is that she just doesn't like the sex she is having (more on this later).

Sometimes, the reason our sex force says "no" is related to trauma. It is extremely common for women to have both direct personal experience of sexual trauma and unhealthy family dynamics around sexuality. You may think you don't have sexual trauma because you haven't personally experienced overt abuse, but a family in which unhealthy dynamics exist, even subtle ones, can unconsciously affect your feelings about sex. While it is beyond the scope of this book to address sexual abuse and trauma, I have provided a great resource section at the end of the book to support you.

Another reason a woman's sex desire becomes hard to wake up is that she doesn't feel happy with the person she is sleeping with. Maybe her partner hasn't been taking out the trash and it's pissing her off. Maybe they've been working long hours, and she resents the fact that they want a quickie late at night when she's already tired. Maybe she secretly thinks they might be cheating, or just watching a ton of porn. There are limitless ways we secretly deny what our deeper, sexual self knows. And rather than admitting these things, it feels safer to keep them buried. But the body doesn't lie, and libido is one of the first places the body will try to communicate the things you're trying to ignore.

A key way to dust off the mirror of your inner resentments is to make a commitment with your partner to take a few moments to clear any relational detritus before having sex. Some of you may be shaking your head right now. "Are you kidding me?" you may be saying. "If I opened up that box of resentment, it could take all night to get through. Not to mention, it could be a major mood killer!"

It is true. It could take all night! But better to clear the air than dampen your sexual force long term. If we want a truly authentic sexual life, we have to be honest with our partners. This may involve getting some couples counseling if the resentment box is really full. But once it's cleared out, any daily resentments can be resolved quickly and easily, making room for deeper intimacy on all levels.

Rajas: Pouncing Tigress Mode

The second stage of our sexual arousal is rajas, or sexual passion. This is the part of sex that is active, athletic, animal, red-blooded, and passionate. It can be fast or slow, but there is movement. Think of it as the ascent of climactic sexual energy.

While there are no hard-and-fast rules, in general, women's bodies often need *way more time* beyond the "waking the sex-cat" first stage of arousal. Men are (usually) different, and have a quicker biological sexual response. Of course, there is a vast spectrum of individual sexual proclivities, but according to ancient Tantra, men hold fire, which burns quickly, and women hold water, which takes its time.

I remember being surprised when the sex educator at The Shakti School, Chris Muse, taught us that it takes about forty-five minutes for the tissues of the vulva to be fully engaged and ready for the greatest amount of pleasure. I thought myself pretty well educated sexually, but I realized that I was not. You see, what we learn from school, religious institutions, our parents, teenage friends, and the media is often not at all aligned with our sexual truth. We often flower into deeper pleasure when we have more touch, flirtation, foreplay, and innuendo outside the scope of sexual penetration. Imagine learning the forty-five-minute thing back in high school sex ed!

Sattva: Glowing Tigress Mode

The last stage—sattva, or sexual lucidity—occurs at the moment of orgasm and after. The French call orgasm *la petite mort*, the little death—not because we die, but because our thinking mind stops. The orgasmic moment holds the potential for pure clarity about ourselves, our partner, and all of life. Temporarily, the goddesses of our animal wildness and our emotional creatrix are both dissolved in a transcendent light, the bliss of sexual pleasure. The climax of orgasm then gives way to a more relaxed place where deep rest and healing can be felt.

This is the resting exhilaration, the deep relaxation of the post-orgasmic response. After our sexual peak, we now experience a valley of relaxation. Think of this stage as a *glowing period* when we get to rest in the fulfillment of desire.

This last part of the wave is too often rushed through. When we think we are "done" with sex, we may rush to roll over, clean up, check our phones, or get up and start the daily grind again. Resist this impulse! Take time to rest in the sacred light your sexual experience has created. Don't sacrifice this place of emotional release and healing at the altar of "getting back to real life." After sex, see if you can hold the last stage as a meditative portal and truly rest in your sexual glow.

SLOW LIKE HONEY

There is value to slowing down at all stages of sex, according to ancient sex traditions. In Ayurveda, sweetness and slowness are the name of the game. There can be great pleasure rewards in learning to go slowly, taking time with the unique body and particular enjoyments of our partner. And remember, many of us experience the sexual response like a slow-building golden honey, whereas others experience it more like a lightning bolt or a blazing fire. As we all know, fire moves faster than honey, so negotiating that balance becomes an important part of intimacy.

A part of taking time may also involve being brave enough to ask for what feels good. It may initially feel easier to stay silent around our sexual longings, but when we do, these secret longings may come out in unhealthy ways. Even worse, if we are touched in ways that don't feel good to our soul, we may end up unconsciously blaming ourselves or deciding sex doesn't feel good in general.

It is okay to give yourself free rein to have a slower build. Educate your lover on what that means for you. Do whatever brings you and your partner pleasure—you can have a quickie in a bathroom if you want to, or you can try for a slower build; both will be appreciated if approached with fun and love. And while of course we're all different and live along a sexual pleasure spectrum, in general it is deeply healing for many women to understand that their deepest sexuality *will take longer*. Give yourself permission to own that fact.

THE ERROR OF "DON'T CATCH FEELINGS"

A woman truly steps into her sexual power when she places value on her deepest heart longings. Pop culture encourages women to pretend they can have sex willy-nilly and see "catching feelings" as something to be avoided. Just as we've been taught the puritanical notion that sex is bad or sinful, or that it's only for one person for the rest of our lives, we are also taught a potentially misleading form of female empowerment that says that the more people you have sex with (without any kind of feelings), the more "empowered" you are.

And many of us know the feeling of acting like a "cool girl" who can have sex without expecting any deeper connection, when what we really want is more long-term. If you really are exploring a sex-capade with no strings attached, great! But it's also okay to acknowledge an intuitive, heart-felt longing for something deeper.

Give yourself permission to take as much or as little time as you want in dating and getting to know someone before you have sex with them. Another wacko trend in movies and TV is the idea that sex tends to happen around date three (or even on date one!). That may work for you—but it may also be helpful to think of yourself as a gatekeeper to your sexual energy. You are allowed to want mental and emotional assurance before sleeping with someone, despite what pop culture may say.

Of course, if you want to have sex with someone on the first date, that's awesome! But it's also okay to give yourself permission to wait a really long time. (And in my experience, men secretly love it!) In fact, I have found that it takes me two to three months to really know if I want to have sex with someone. Remember, a sexual partner holds the most intimate aspect of you. "Take your time" is not a bad mantra.

GIVE SEX SPACE

Another key component of keeping sexual energy alive is in *differentiation*. Modern culture has romantic partners living on top of each other. We share a bed and a bathroom, and think our sexual partner needs to be our best friend, baby daddy or mama, and sex guru. That's a lot to ask from one person!

Differentiation is a way of creating sexual space. Men can experience an increase in testosterone when they get their space, which may provide scientific credence for the value of the infamous "man cave." But men aren't the only ones who need their space. Having time and room for your solo self provides an opportunity for women to recharge their creative energy, too.

Imagine a world where couples sleep in separate parts of the house and meet in the middle to connect during the day. For the first three and a half weeks of the month, they are encouraged to flirt outrageously, listen to music, adorn themselves with beautiful jewels, clothing, and scents, dine together, give each other little gifts, speak sweet naughty nothings into one another's ears, and in general sexually tease the you-know-what out of each other. Then, when they can barely take it any longer, the last three days of the month they never leave their love-making bedroom. This is what some ancient sex teachings recommended for marital bliss!

WHO GETS TO BE INSIDE OUR SEX AURA?

Another big part of becoming sexually empowered involves making good decisions about who we let deeper into the field of our sexual body. The ancient teachings are clear: In sexual exchanges, we exchange parts of ourselves that go beyond the body. In other words, we take our partner into us—not just physically but energetically. For this reason, we want to think about being good energy gatekeepers to the door of our sexual life.

I remember one of my mentors telling me, "When you sleep with someone, ask yourself the question, 'Do I want to become like this person?' Because you will begin to share his karma."

I know, right?!

Now, that's not meant to scare us. We exchange energy with people every day. But the sexual self is the most intimate self, so it may help to think of dating as interviewing someone for the job of not only holding your heart, but also receiving the most valuable creative force on the planet—your sex power. This has nothing to do with how many dates you go on, or whether or not the person is your one true forever love. This is about taking enough of a Holy Pause around sex to know if the other person is worthy of your intimacy. Plus, we all know that as soon as you start sleeping with someone, emotions and unconscious patterns tend to bubble up, and afterwards you may not be able to see the person you are dating with the clearest of eyes.

One of my favorite concepts in Ayurvedic medicine is the concept of *tarpaka kapha*. This ancient wisdom tradition sees your very flesh as the storehouse of not only your past experiences, but also your lineage. It delineates different types of tissues and the ways in which these tissues store both your and your ancestors' memories. Tarpaka kapha is the white matter of your brain, your cerebrospinal fluids, and the sexual fluids your body emits when you are turned on or orgasm. Ancient Ayurveda believed that your deepest memories are stored, dormant, in these tissues and fluids. When you engage sexually with someone, whether with intimate massage, kissing, or full-on intercourse, you activate these ancient memories in both yourself and your partner.

For this reason, I think of sex as nuclear energy. It supercharges whatever we are holding in our unconscious mind and heart. It opens the doorway to both our deepest traumas and our untapped capacity for universal love. When we use it wisely, we can bring to light all of our unconscious material, giving us the opportunity to lovingly reframe and heal the past. Love for our partner, like love for ourselves, can act as a digestive enzyme on the old content that sex's nuclear power awakens. Love helps us sort through all the old emotional baggage that comes up between us and our partners.

When we are in a great, healthy relationship, we can trust the container of our partnership to be able to hold all that awakened content. We can use this sexual nuclear energy to blow up our lives in the best of ways—by co-creating our future reality, through encouraging one another to do the individual work of healing and awakening to our souls. When we don't know how to use this nuclear energy, however, or we sex it up with someone who is toxic for our soul's journey, it can blow up our lives.

STOP LEAKING YOUR SEXY

We leak our sexual energy when we use it to manipulate others and/or get external validation of our intrinsic worth through sex. There is nothing sexier than a woman whose energy flows inside her body (the kind of woman the great energy-based internalizing meditations in this book will help you become!). From that inner flow, she is able to give the overflow.

So how do we stop leaking our sexual energy? We realize that we have to be tuned in to our soul in order to have a real soul meeting with another. We bring awareness to the deeper longing inside our sexual impulses. We pause and check in with ourselves before acting, asking, *What is my real intention?*

Am I coming from love or from lack? Am I celebrating my sexuality, creativity, and relationships from a place of overflow or a place of lack? Am I moving from a place of trusting my soul's journey, or trying to manipulate reality from a place of faithlessness? We stop leaking our sexual energy, usually over time, through a slow awakening to all the ways we've used our bodies to get what we may be terrified we don't have within.

Nothing kills the holiness of sex quicker than games of control, narcissism, codependency, suppression, or blame. As our self-love, self-confidence, and depth of spiritual life increase, a deeper, glowing sexiness can emerge. This sexiness has nothing to do with youth or the amount of wrinkles on your skin or the shape of your body, but a willingness to be with every holy aspect of yourself—to luxuriate in your light. There is nothing sexier than confidence, real vulnerability, and the ability to be with life as it is without conditions.

Lastly, whether we are single or partnered, when we leak our sexuality, we will eventually feel unfulfilled. And when we feel unfulfilled, our energy body—the aura that surrounds us, which is normally glowing gold and pink—begins to turn gray. And trust me, there have been many periods in my life, including many that I've written about in this book, when I've gone gray. My longing for myself, and for you, is that we *stay glowing gold and pink.*

TIPS ON STAYING GLOWING GOLD AND PINK

I'm not a fan of hard-and-fast rules and how-to lists when it comes to the act of sex. In a truly tolerant and wise world, everyone would understand the guiding laws of sexual energy while at the same time understanding sexual diversity and fluidity. Many ancient societies understood sexualized spirit energy deeply, and they knew that endless variation was the way of nature! But whether you are pleasuring yourself alone or with another, sex should be fun, deeply intimate, and personal. Sex should be considered sacred ground.

With that, here are a few basic "holy sex tips" based on decades of study in Ayurveda, Taoism, sacred women's practices, mentorship work, and my own "stumbling-toward-enlightenment" life.

1. **You are in charge.** No one should tell you what to do or how to feel about your sex life. That's your job. That is why, for me, it felt *so yuck* to have some guy in a suit at a pulpit tell me what to do with one of the most personal and sacred aspects of my being. It's the same reason it feels creepy to have some dude tell you he has the secret "only way" that you should know God. Most things done in the sex realm between consenting adults are fair game.

2. **The womb and breasts, by nature, absorb things.** In Ayurveda, we understand the womb to have the superpower of holding things— good and bad, physical and emotional, personal and collective. It also creates, nurtures, and gives of itself. This is one of the reasons it is so critical to keep the lymphatic tissue of the womb, as well as the breasts, clear: They have a particular affinity for absorbing toxins. (This absorptive ability is why when you drink too much caffeine you may notice effects on your breast tissue and your period!) On an energetic level, the womb space mirrors physical reality. It is very easy for our wombs to take on the undigested emotions of our entire household and channel them out as PMS symptoms. (For more information on this, consult the resources section on The Shakti School programs.)

3. **Value your sensual and sexual pleasure.** When we devalue our deep need for fulfilling sex (in favor of our busy lives, calendars, careers, and other people)—when we value *only* taking care of others over our own pleasure and deep contentment—this imbalance can show up in covert ways, such as irritability, overwhelm, or exhaustion. Start to notice inner signals of ease and pleasure throughout the day. By noticing the little things in life—the smell of coffee, the feeling of a cold wintery morning, the taste of a perfect grapefruit—we start to fill up our pleasure tanks on natural, non-addictive, life-giving delights. This translates to the bedroom.

4. **Love heals.** When you are working with your sexual energy, one simple question to ask yourself is, "Will what I am about to do bring more love and goodness into my life and the world, or more pain?" Wait and let your intuition speak to you.

5. **Muscles are what give our bodies the ability to have fulfilling sex.** One of the best things we can do for our sex lives is to start lifting weights and eating clean. Often our culture sees men as sexually vital when they are strong and healthy, and women as sexually valuable when they are thin, small, demure, and young. The ancients understood the value of a woman developing her *muscles*. In fact, in ancient Ayurveda, the muscles are an important part of the sexual body and a fountain of vitality as we age. You are not the age of your years, you are the age of how much functional muscle you have. Don't believe me? Check out Ernestine Shepherd, the oldest female body builder. She is well into her 80s and sexy as hell.

6. **Grow the power of your focus.** You won't get mind-blowing sex without being able to hold deep concentration. When you are able to stay centered inside your body and meditate on your pleasure, you can enter into a sex ecstasy that involves every cell of your being. How do you grow sexual concentration power? Believe it or not, the Holy Pause and the meditation on the five senses (see page 57) is one of the best ways to do it.

7. **Dry brush and self-massage.** The ancients used the word *sneha* to refer to both "oil" and "love." Regularly touching your body with oil helps promote a connection to it, aiding you in knowing and loving your body in a way that can immediately translate into the bedroom. Plus, when we massage ourselves, we access our fascia, muscle, and fat tissue. When we do it with love, self-massage has the capacity to purify cellular memory and activate a magnetism that draws in the sexual life you are truly worthy of.

8. **Become a tactile kitty cat.** After several years of practicing orienting my senses to the outside world as well as cultivating the tactile sense of my own body, I began to activate my dormant sensory neurons. With practice, I could experience more and more sensual pleasure from seemingly nonsexual things. I would run my hand down the stair banister and feel a ripple of yumminess run through my body. I would feel the sensation of grass in my fingertips and wonder how I'd never noticed how pleasurable plants were. I would notice the feel of

my pants like buttery softness. It was as if regular life was suddenly full of opportunities for healthy, life-affirming, micro-pleasures.

9. **Engage in exercises that mimic coital movements.** Snakelike movement builds your inner sexual energy and sensual pleasure. These movements help you uncover new sensations, vibrations, and interrelated dimensions inside your body. Why do you think they banned dancing in church?! (If you want some examples, head to my website for a members-only platform full of energy-building movement practices for awakening this snake-like force.)

10. **See yourself and your lover through the eyes of God.** As you make love, learn to pendulate between meditating on the pleasure inside your own body from receiving sexual stimulation and the pleasure of giving to another. See your partner and yourself as holy beings, divine creatures. See your lovemaking as a reenactment of the original creation story—where pure consciousness and pure energy reunite!

A GLOW-WORTHY MEDITATION
Light-Filled

I want to share one more energy practice with you. This again comes from my work with Cristal Mortensen. Through our work together, I have learned that anxiety and stress are a sign that we don't have enough energy, not that we have too much! So, first, we want to drop our energy down the back of our body. Then we want to drop that energy into our own inner body.

Start with the practice in the Energy chapter on page 81 (the waterfall meditation) to become connected to life-force energy, followed by the practice in the Wounds chapter on page 135 to ground yourself. The practice that follows is the third step. In it, we begin to pull energy up from the earth into our body. This experience of being present in both our own bodies and the earth is what allows us to truly be "grounded."

This last energy practice will help you truly fill up and rest in the experience of being both grounded and full of life, helping you both contain your energy and build it.

As we have done before, feel your attention and energy drop down from the top of the head, through the middle of it. Now, down through the throat, heart and hands, belly, abdomen, and down through the legs. All the way down to the soles of your feet.

You may need to do this a few times to feel that you have fully arrived in and down in your own body.

Once you feel that sense of inner grounding, now you can begin to feel your awareness moving down into earth energy. For me, it helps to bring my attention to the soles of my feet and make contact with the earth energy. What does this energy of the earth below me feel like?

Without overthinking it, just tune your attention to the energy of earth.

Then, below your feet, sense the earth energy coming up into you— almost as if you are actively pulling earth energy into your body. If it helps, you can feel it come through the soles of your feet.

As you inhale, feel it rise all the way up through your body, and as you exhale, feel it fill you up and even expand all around you.

It's that simple. On the inhale, pull earth energy up through your whole body, and on the exhale, feel it plump you up, moving even beyond the boundary of your physical skin.

Continue to inhale and exhale in this way, pulling earth energy into you and feeling it fill and hold you.

12

Hell Yes

By this point in the book, you have realized the deep importance of not shying away from pain, primal sexuality, emotions, and other inner experiences our society has made taboo. Remembering our glow-worthiness requires us to be with all of ourselves.

So, you get it—it is vitally important not to run from yourself—and this means all the feelings you would rather not feel.

But that is not all we are called to do. We are also called to step into praise, positivity, and co-creation with the goodness of life. There is no technique that adds God to our experience, only subtraction methods that remove the obstacles to the glowing light that is already within us. Praise and celebration are activation methods that remind us that life indeed is beautiful. And we always have something to be grateful for.

Simply stated, God wants us to party.

We—and I'm definitely including me here—tend to alternate between two polarized ways of relating to our emotions. First, there is the aspect of us that is a worrywart. Our worrywart self can get obsessed with a painful past, endlessly reliving it, wallowing in dark feelings and thoughts, failing to see the endless beautiful possibilities of the future. When we are in worrywart mode, we are constantly scanning the past or future for things to be afraid of and trying to control the future so we don't experience pain again.

Then there is our inner pain-denier. This is the part of all of us that just refuses to acknowledge any of our unsavory parts, or the unsavoriness of others. This denial leads us to focus only on the positives, or the parts of us that we like and identify with. This is a kind of "toxic positivity" whereby we deny suffering in ourselves, others, and the world so we don't have to feel it within.

But toxic positivity is not real positivity at all. Real positivity is full of love. It never denies the full spectrum of life's emotional experience. Real love is a good parent. It allows us to feel our emotions, sensations, and experiences in the moment and then guides us toward the sunshine and goodness of *what could be tomorrow.*

It is our job to find balance between both of these polarities—positive and negative. In previous chapters we honored and worked with our inner darkness and the pain of returning to our own psychic underworld. In this chapter, we will focus on *how to become a magnet for good things to come to you and through you.* In this way, it's possible to become both an attractor for blessing and a bestower of blessings on everyone else.

Hell yes. And hallelujah.

SOUL ROLE CALL

The more we are present and free from expectations, the more we can sense the call of the soul. The more we clean up our own inner world, the more open we are to channeling Divine will, which is another way of saying the pull of our own highest Self. The more we digest our karma (our unresolved emotions, outdated perceptions, and drama-producing reactions), the more our current actions can produce more wholesome, soul-filled fruit. And the more grateful we are to just be here, on Earth, learning all these lessons, the more we attract things that bring us even deeper into our Divine birthright. And that is *freedom.*

In your daily life, when you honor your spiritual glow and do the practices that help you stay in the power of loving presence, the teachings of Tantra say that you become imbued with *sankalpa shakti,* the indomitable will of magnetic intention. When you stay connected to the God of your own heart, in whatever way feels deeply authentic to you, the Christian tradition says you become a carrier of a "commanded blessing."

Take that in for a moment. When you get your heart right with yourself (self-love) and your heart right with a Higher Power, you are filled with something that *commands* power and blessings to come into your life. That means less trying, more receiving. Less effort, more abundance. Less energy, more return.

Sign. Me. Up.

But how do we get in that right alignment with the Divine? Well, this whole book is a map. But this section in particular is about how to become a *lightning rod for God.* And trust me, I know this stuff works, because I am *not* naturally positive all the time! Left to my own devices, I have a tendency to ruminate on negative thoughts. I am, as they say in India, full of worry, hurry, and too much curry. I can also easily get caught up in my negative emotions and body sensations and confuse them with the bigger truth of reality. Because of that, cultivating the vibes of "hell yeahs and hallelujahs" has been a critical piece in my spiritual practice.

Imagine that a higher force has placed a blessing magnet inside us. But the Divine won't force this magnetic attractor of goodness upon us; instead, we have to invite it in. The Tantric teachings say that if we want Lakshmi (the goddess of true abundance) to show up, *we need to become like her.* Her abundance is always available, but it is up to us to clear our vision to be able to experience it.

In other words, if you want abundance, feel how much richness already exists in your life. If you want sexiness, walk around like you have diamonds between your legs. If you want to feel your intrinsic health, marvel at how much your body has been through and how you are still here. This isn't about denying the moments when you may not feel this way—sometimes we are deep in debt, our libido's low, or we have the flu! It's about allowing ourselves to be open to receiving all aspects of reality—both the challenges *and* the gifts.

In my own spiritual life, I think of this as a co-creation with the Divine. My job in the partnership is to live my daily nonnegotiables—the daily self-care and spiritual practices I do in order to keep my body and mind as healthy as possible—and to remain with a trusting heart. I wake up and, before turning on my phone, do my sacred readings, prayers, and meditations. I listen to positive, life-affirming podcasts, talks, and music. I get my daily food plan in order. I exercise. I watch my words, especially how I talk to myself about myself. I ask the Divine to live with me. And I take *a lot* of Holy Pauses. Some days, I have to say the Holy Pause just a few times a day. On rough days, sometimes it seems I have to repeat it on every other breath.

Staying in a trusting heart means trusting the wisdom within the process of our life. As long as we are living from within our intuition, doing our best to work with our energy in a positive way, and rectifying things when we mess up (which will happen!), we can trust that all things are working for the eventual good. This can be challenging, because the healing process often looks like two steps forward, one back. When our body is healing, it often becomes more painful and inflamed before it finally heals. It's the same with our spiritual life.

FIVE PRACTICES FOR BECOMING A LIGHTNING ROD FOR SOUL BLESSINGS

Tuning in to your inner soul-call will make you more aware of the right people, opportunities, and seemingly magical resources. Some of them may already be in your life! You won't have to work as hard at your creations. World-changing ideas, books, poems, and music *will come to you and through you*. That is the result of becoming a magnet. The more genuine life- and love-affirming thoughts fill your mind, the more you will become an unstoppable force for blessings. Here are some practices that will get you started in electrifying that lightning rod of soul blessings.

Hell Yes Practice #1: Orienting to Goodness

Neuroscientists have discovered that when we complain and focus on the negative, it actually wires our brains for a more negative perspective. And although our biological bias toward negativity does work to keep us safe and hypervigilant, always looking for the thing to fear, flee, or fight unfortunately makes our modern life feel really hard. Shifting to a neutral or positive outlook is like lifting weights for your brain. For many of us, it's like learning a new skill.

In almost every moment, our mind has the capacity to notice what is right and what is good in what we already have. *What is already given.* How often do we take the most basic comfy, cozy things in our life for granted? Another simple way we can activate our neural networks of praise is by loving not only ourselves and the people in our lives, but the rooms and objects we live in and with on a daily basis. Yes, loving up the very space you find yourselves in. That means, your kitchen, living room, office, backyard, car . . . wherever you spend your time. As the saying goes, "What you appreciate, appreciates"—that is, what you pay loving attention to can grow.

Rather than seeing what's wrong, missing, or uncomfortable, what would your life be like if you spent at least 50 percent of your time thinking and feeling about what was absolutely right? Shifting your attention to what is pleasurable and good can be life-changing.

One of my favorite ways of moving into sensory appreciation is to touch things. Of all the senses, the tactile sense is one of the best ways we can deeply ground our nervous system in the material world, as it calls for the least amount of separation between us and the object we are engaging with. Try noticing the softness of the clothing you love the most. It can also feel really nice to let your bare feet feel the pleasing rough texture of the rug underneath. My mom's house has a velvet chair that makes my senses tingle. Other women I know enjoy the soothingly abrasive quality of a wicker chair back.

✳ A GLOW-WORTHY MEDITATION ✳
Beholding the Goodness

Right now, what is absolutely right about your world? Take a moment to pause and let your eyes wander about the room. Notice where your eyes are

*naturally drawn. What colors feel soothing and pleasing? What do you notice
in your immediate environment that you appreciate? Spend the moment
with an object you find particularly agreeable. Don't judge the experience.*

*My eyes are often drawn to a turquoise label on a water bottle
in my kitchen. I don't know why—my senses just like it. This
is a body-based form of appreciation and knowingness.*

*Let agreeableness and pleasure register within your body. How long
does it take before you get pulled into the world of thoughts?*

*You can do this with any of the five senses. What
do you hear? Smell? Taste? Feel?*

Let each of your senses really land in the body before moving on.

Hell Yes Practice #2: Dance, Sing, and Celebrate Like Your Life Depends on It

Our soul responds to energetic pulses, music, rhythm, and life-affirming words. This is why so many religions, healers, and shamanic traditions involve the beat of a drum, the power of music, and the repetition of positive, life-affirming sounds and mantras. The music and praise we create on the inside help our soul feel that the body is a positive, loving, blessed place to return to. This isn't just a spiritual truth that existed in the past, it is a living biological experience that brings belonging and blessing.

Think of the soul's blessings as heat-seeking missiles. Celebratory dance and song make your body hot. When you work your body and energy into more heat and light, and add to that a positive intention, thought, and feeling, the missiles of blessing are like, "Oh, hey, hot mama! I'm coming at you!" Simply stated—blessings can find you more easily when you are in that radiant light of celebration.

This is the ultimate activation of your intrinsic light.

You may be titillated to hear that some of the first churches had no pews. Legend holds that people had ecstatic proto-Christian dance parties inside these early churches, whipping themselves into a hot God-frenzy. And today we still see this celebratory force in many Black and Pentecostal churches. Perhaps the rest of us lost this tradition because the powers that be saw that the attendees were becoming too powerful and unwieldly, and promptly installed those punishing pews that numb your bum and extinguish the holy body-ecstasy.

Moving your body and proclaiming the goodness in your life through your voice isn't New Agey, "just practice *The Secret*" kinda stuff. It's a fully embodied power move for getting a more magical life. Singing and dancing together in community is mental health first aid. This isn't a primitive practice. It's a human requirement.

Still think it's a little woo? Scientific studies have confirmed the neurophysiological benefits of praise, dance, positivity, and proclaiming goodness for yourself, your life, and your family. Sonja Lyubomirsky, in her book *The How of Happiness: A New Approach to Getting the Life You Want*, puts it this way: "Gratitude is an antidote to negative emotions, a neutralizer of envy, hostility, worry, and irritation."

Other research has shown that communal, gratitude-giving activities such as praise and worship downregulate the amygdala and hypothalamus, the parts of the brain largely involved in the reactive fight-or-flight response. And when the amount of time a person spends in that chronic stress state is reduced, their body shows a decrease in heart rate, blood pressure, blood glucose levels, and markers of inflammation. The effects of praise, dance, and worship aren't only physical—these practices can reduce depression, anxiety, chronic pain, and PTSD.

As we proclaim, profess, and otherwise verbally call in goodness, we boost the density of the neurons in our brain that support a positive mindset. This mindset can then flow like healing honey throughout the rest of the body, while the neural circuits for gratitude in the brain are reinforced, making it more likely that your brain will seek positivity without you trying!

Singing and dancing, particularly with others, activates our physiology in such a way that it dissolves our sense of separation from the world. When we move in celebration and positive affirmation, we begin to dissolve the pain that comes from feeling alone and different. Sacred praise and movement help our brain connect with something bigger than our limited sense of self, and augment our sense of belonging to something beyond our fears, worries, and personality quirks.

We heal anxiety and depression through the physiology of deep belonging. No social media site can ever replace the ecstatic, healing union of actual flesh-and-blood companionship and sacred group ritual. There is a reason why Catholic mass, Baptist holy-rolling praise dance, choirs, and tribal dance exist. They are radical acts that join us together in the reality of our shared pain. This nests us within the common humanity we share, allowing us to heal through both feeling that pain and transmuting it.

You don't have to be esoteric and fancy about it. You also don't have to be churchy about it. Just put on some booty-grooving music you love. Let the beat move you, get a little sweat going on, and when you feel the heat and energy rising in your body, raise your hands in the air and yell out, "Hell yes!" (Or, if you want a PG version, use my friend Mer's mantra, "Yay day!"—as in, today is a good day!) Keep moving and thanking God, Buddha, Jesus, the Universe, or whoever you keep in your God-pocket. Just move and breathe and dance in a spirit of *thank you*.

Hell Yes Practice #3: Speak Blessings, Not Curses

The idea of blessings—of speaking favor over myself and my life, either silently or aloud—is one of the most potent practices from the tradition I grew up in. But blessings don't just include the words and objects you receive from God. They are also quiet prayers you can launch into your life. Think of these as *inner* blessings—words, like spells, that you cast into your future.

The proclamations, prophecies, and blessings you speak over your life are a powerful lightning rod for God. The secret here is to feel as if what you are saying and praying for is *already done, already here*. This is the tried-and-true heart of all manifestation methodology. Take a moment now to notice: Are you blessing yourself? Or are you in a mind state of negativity, contraction, and critique? It's okay if you are! Just noticing how often we are in this kind of mind state starts to shift our inner dialogue from fear into presence.

Singing and speaking words of praise, gratitude, and healing (whether out loud or not) has been shown to increase pleasure-inducing chemicals like dopamine and serotonin. But praise is not just about *feeling* gratitude—these benefits also arise when we *express* that gratitude through our words and actions toward others.

My mom and I speak at least a few times a week. We fill each other in on the goings-on in both of our lives, getting updates on the nieces and nephews and what's happening in the neighborhood. But we also do a fair amount of bitching. One day my mom had a really great idea. She said, "Wow, I'm feeling so negative. What would it be like if we told each other ten things that were actually really great in our lives?"

I'm not going to lie—part of me thought this was a little bit cheesy, especially doing it with my mom. But I went with it.

She went first: "I really love my house, and I'm so grateful to have a soft comfy bed to sleep in."

Then I said, "I am so glad that I have my health and so much love and support around me through my staff, family, and friends."

And back and forth we went until each of us had said ten things that we were really happy about and grateful for. Ten things that we loved about our lives. By the end of those twenty statements, my mom and I both felt a palpable, visceral lift in our mood. It was way better than our usual bitch-fests.

In his seminal research on couples and happiness, John Gottman found that for every one negative interaction a couple had, they needed to have five positive ones in order to have a lasting, fulfilled relationship. So, it's an easy formula to tip the scales in the direction of becoming a blessings magnet: one part cathartic bitch-fest, five parts powerful, positive speech and divine proclamations.

You can try it now. Just put down this book and take a moment to speak, out loud, what is "going right" in your life. You can also find a friend to do this practice with. Instead of only talking about the stuff that's hard in our lives (which, by the way, is still something we need to do with one another), commit to spending most of the conversation talking about what can be celebrated and praised about your lives. Notice what starts to happen to your mood.

Hell Yes Practice #4: Remember Who the Divine Says You Are

When I am feeling low, it is really helpful to remember who the Divine says I am. I may *feel* sad, lonely, and a little PMS-y, but *my true self isn't any of those things.*

Below are a series of affirmative truths about who you truly are. They are my own God-truths, which I have collected over the past twenty years from a variety of religious traditions. Feel free to create your own, based on your own traditions, intuitions, and rituals.

Simply reading these mantras will *not* be enough to alter you. This is not an exercise to do with your conscious mind. It requires engaging your emotions, using visualization, and, most importantly, getting your whole body involved.

Some of these ancient spiritual truths may not feel like they fit. Some of them may even completely turn you off! So how can you start to feel these ancient spiritual truths if the statements feel way off to you at this moment?

There's a trick to it: *You have to first feel it,* and then believing is easy. Begin each sentence with, "What would it feel like, right here and now in my body, if I believed X with every cell of my being?" So the first one would read, "What would it feel like, right here and now in my body, if I really believed with all of my heart that *my true nature is whole and complete?*"

Let's try it.

** A GLOW-WORTHY CONTEMPLATION ****

Felt Affirmations

Speak each of the following affirmations, really allowing them to be *felt* by the body. You can do one a day, or try out a few right now to see which ones are most meaningful. Which really resonate? Which are more challenging to feel? This is a great guidance system on which parts of you may still need healing.

What would it feel like if I knew, in my whole body that...

I am whole and complete.

I am a branch on the vine of creation—I am full of the same essence as all of creation.

I am joyful.

I am wanted.

I am wise in spirit.

I am forgiven.

I am, with every breath, a new creation, not a victim of my past.

I am light.

I am love.

I am free from condemnation.

I am the temple of the Divine.

I was created to do beautiful things in the world.

I have a holy calling.

I have boldness and confidence.

I am safe in spirit, no matter the outer circumstances.

The Divine guards my heart and mind in peace.

I am already healed.

I am like a tree planted by water: Whatever I do will bear fruit.

I am radiant, flawless.

I am never alone.

I am more than enough in spirit.

I am blessed in spirit.

I am a citizen of bliss and peace.

I am created for thoughts of peace, prosperity, and hope for a brighter future.

I am beautiful like the moon and even brighter than the stars.

Hell Yes Practice #5: Swaha, Aho, Amen (aka Let That Shit Go)

Think of your future dreams as your babies. In order to birth these cosmic dreams into the material realm, we need a fertile womb. How do we get a fertile womb on the energetic and spiritual level? Perhaps the most important thing we seem to always forget is that bringing a dream to fruition, like having a baby, is not just about what we do (aka, having sex), it's also about our capacity to relax and receive—and about feeling safe enough to do both of those things.

I can't tell you how many women I've worked with who tried everything to get pregnant. Doing, doing, doing, taking all the herbs, getting fertility treatments, hormones, all the things . . . only to give up, go on vacation with their man, and get pregnant just when they had finally let it go.

It's the same with our dreams. While planning and doing are vitally important to materializing life ambitions, it's even more important to *relax*, trust Divine timing, and be chilled out enough in the vessel of our body to receive what is coming to and through us.

I like to say that I work hard, and then I lie around like a lazy tigress. True dream-queens know how to lounge. And rest. And let go of the expectation of ever getting exactly what they want, while trusting in the bigger soul-calling that is occurring.

Sometimes that is hard. I get it. There are times when I know I need to relax, but I am so wound up and so in my head that it's hard to get there. We have to go to the body—the feeling center of our awareness—to get the ease. And the body needs a little time.

Especially if you continue to practice them over time, the meditations in this book will help you get there. For those of you who want a little more guidance, I created an entire year-long program and a video/audio subscription platform to hold you in these practices. You can access it at www.theshaktischool.com.

13

Light

Okay, beautiful person—I hope that by this point in the book, you've been inspired to cultivate the two most important relationships of your life:

1. **The relationship between you and you.** A good sign that this relationship is going well is a deeper sense of loving appreciation for yourself—both your past self with all her messy moments and the you that you are becoming.

2. **Your relationship with something bigger than you, that will always be there to support you.** Another good sign that this relationship is going well is a feeling that no matter what happens, there's a benevolent force holding you—a feeling that you aren't alone anymore.

As these relationships become more and more a central focal point for your life, you access more of your inner light. You also get better at learning how to hold that light, which in turn expresses itself as a glow from within. It's that simple. There is a reason our ancient ancestors called the spiritual path and goal en*light*enment. You are literally getting more *in light*. And light can hold it all—even your darkest stuff.

Each of the preceding chapters of this book taught you how to connect with the light inside of you. This chapter will allow us to *contain* and *respect* this light. With all the practice you've done, you've worked your focus pretty hard to awaken your light and subsequently feel your true inner glowing. In this chapter, you'll continue to learn how to keep that newly cultivated light radiating steadily.

You see, it's like a sweet little baby, this light. We have to hold it, feed it, and keep it away from bad stuff. Most importantly, this chapter will help you learn how to safe-keep this sacred light—not by running from bullies or hiding in a cave, but by walking boldly into battle, like a Goddess riding a tiger.

YOUR GLOW-WORTHY LIGHT

What exactly is this inner light we should be so invested in awakening and protecting?

The oral Tantric tradition of both Hinduism and Buddhism likens this light inside each of us to a sacred and special jewel called a *mani*. This gem is not like a normal diamond or ruby that requires an outside source to reflect light. This is a gem that is self-effulgent. It needs nothing but itself to fully shine. It is both self-illuminating and self-regenerating. It is infinitely glowing *in and of itself.*

And guess what? *That gem is the real you.* Not the broken you. The effed-up you. The scattered you. The scared you. The doubting you. It's the real you. Innocent, yet wise. A light unto itself.

✴ A GLOW-WORTHY CONTEMPLATION ✴
This Little Light of Mine

Inside each of us is an impenetrable light of spirit, untouched
by the things that have happened to us in our past, even the

*really bad stuff. It is untouched by our trauma, untainted by
our ancestors' pain, and unaffected by our addictions.*

*Take that in for a moment. Maybe even say it out loud, letting
the following words resonate into the cells of your body:*

*Inside me I have an inner light that can fuel and guide me. I need nothing
other than this light to know what to do next. This light can soothe me.
Heal me. Awaken me. This light is the source of my true self-esteem.
This light is both innately pure and immensely powerful. This light can
connect to an endless source of an even bigger light all around me.*

THE DUST ON OUR LIGHT

The teachings say that *everyone* has this light-filled gem. It lives in our hearts, safeguarded inside a crystalline box. When we are young, this box is clear and pristine and the light can shine brightly, illuminating who we really are to everyone around us. That's why little kids are so fun to be around. They are like little light-boxes, being completely and totally themselves. Even when they are angry or sad, there is a sacred realness about children that most of us instinctively know we must protect.

Sadly, with time, the light we project often begins to dim. It's not because the light itself dims, but because the crystalline box gets coated in a layer of dust. This dusting of our light-box happens whenever someone does or says something to us that diminishes us and causes an inner disconnection. Shame, trauma, harsh words, and other forms of abuse create a thick coating on our little box. But it's not just traumatic experiences that can block our light. Our overly brash and stimulating world sometimes leads us to create a barrier of self-protection that hides our light. Some kids are just really sensitive, and their boxes tend to get coated the most. In essence, our box becomes dusty any time we forget or deny who we really are.

I remember getting a big dusting on my light-box when I rode the school bus for the first time. I got on in a new outfit my mama had bought me. Now, granted, it *was* a weird balloon-shaped polka-dotted onesie, but my mama told me I looked "cool."

As I made my way down the aisle, I heard a voice yell in my direction from the very back of the bus.

"You look like a fat blimp!" the bully belted out, standing up in the middle of the aisle, pointing his finger directly at me. It was so loud, that voice. The entire bus started giggling at my blimp suit.

Humiliated, I blushed and crouched down in the first seat in the first row—the seat where all the dorks sat. (And the seat I would occupy for the rest of the year, hoping to hide from that boy and his mean mouth.)

But his words didn't leave me. The words "you look like a fat blimp" and the ensuing laughter spun around and around in my head all day. By the time I got home, I collapsed in a heap of tears on my mama's living room couch. I felt totally ashamed.

It's not just other individuals that can dim our light. Aspects of society, culture, and religion—infrastructures that are meant to uplift and edify us—can also teach us that we are something other than innately glow-worthy.

I also don't mean to make my bully out to be a bad guy. We have all been that bully at some point, knowingly or not. The more I learn about my own brain and my own reactions, the more I wonder how many of my own words have unintentionally hurt others. We too cause dust on the boxes of others, often unconsciously. This is a part of all human relationships.

As the dust builds and builds, our luminous gem can become completely obscured. And over time, the dust can turn to sludge. Unfortunately, you can't clean sludge with a feather duster. It must be cleansed with fire.

Fire is the heat and light of our loving presence. It is the protective, wildly compassionate quality of an awakened spiritual life that actually changes you, that melts you and turns what is unneeded into holy, nutritive ash. If we want to have more light, we have to find our light. *Light awakens more light.*

The Buddhist tradition calls spiritual practice "taking refuge." Taking refuge is the consistent discipline of protecting your spiritual light. We can take refuge in whatever spiritual path we choose, but the idea is that there is a place where we can lay our weary human head and feel the deep protection all around us.

Ironically, the more we become protective defenders of our own spiritual light, the less defensive we become. The more fiercely we anchor ourselves to our spiritual light, the stronger we become and the more immune we are to getting new dust on our light-box.

Taking refuge also means not waiting for others to make us feel lovable, safe, or worthy. Sure, a great teacher, mentor, therapist, or friend can *really* help with a box coated in sludge. But inevitably, it is up to each of us to find that inner sacred relationship that fuels the fire of our return to the sacred realness of our youth. It is up to us to become our own safe haven. But this takes time and, yes, a certain amount of effort.

PROTECTING YOUR LIGHT

Whenever I think about spiritual protection, I always think of the great Hindu Goddess Durga.

The best-known teaching on this Goddess comes from the fifth-century myth of the *Devi Mahatmyam* (*Triumph of the Goddess*). In this story, holy hell has broken out on Earth because a bull-demon named Mahishasura has, with his massive ego, taken over. He thinks he is the biggest, baddest, greatest thing to ever happen to the world and constantly announces it on Twitter (okay, I added that part). Caring only about himself, he stomps about creating hate, fear, and division among the people wherever he goes.

Eventually, through the inevitable twists and turns of all great Hindu myths, Durga is able to finally defeat the bull-demon. But she doesn't do it through force or control. She doesn't do it through great feats of violence, or yelling or shaming the bull until he submits to her will. She also doesn't do it by putting on a blindfold and just pretending the bull doesn't exist. She defeats Mahishasura by placing the delicate, soft underbelly of her foot on his throat. Then, with her sword, she pierces his heart, and he is changed. It is with her softness that she supports the bull in transforming himself into light.

What tames the bull inside all of us? It is our own warm, grounded presence. When we hold our own inner demons captive with our focused tenderness, we too have the capacity to become Durga, piercing through the heart of our past pain and transmuting even the most horrific of our own memories into light.

The name Durga means "Impenetrable Fortress." Think of her like a wall of sacred protection all around you. But this wall isn't built from bricks and harsh words, but rather from a soft membrane of fierce, unending love.

Love is invisible. We can't see it, but we know it when we feel it. And it is precisely love's invisibility that lends it its power. Durga does not derive her power from defending herself, but through a relentless commitment to her own inner light, which is the same as loving presence. In fact, one of her other names is the Goddess of Light. And by connecting to your own ability to be loving with all your inner demons, you can also bring light to your most vulnerable parts, as well as the world outside you.

You don't have to buy a statue of Durga, chant her mantras, or become Hindu to connect to this force. She is an archetype within all beings, an energetic signature of the fierce love embodied in us all. She is the true meaning of putting on the protection of light. She is remaining steady in your light, while being aware that doing so may feel like you are riding a tiger on the battlefield of life. She represents, ultimately, the realization that the battle we think we are fighting with our outside enemies is really a war within ourselves.

Let's take a look at some practical, lifestyle-based ways that we can embody this energetic signature, so it can help us hold and protect our light.

BRINGING LIGHT TO THE MIND

Embodying the guardianship of your own inner light means working with the power of your thoughts and reactions. Do you ever notice a steady stream of negative self-talk that can sometimes feel like an endless loop playing in your brain? Consciously choosing to entertain thoughts that build and support you (rather than freak you out and tear you down) is a great way to begin to protect your light.

The Hindu sacred text the *Bhagavad Gita* symbolically likens a human being to a chariot. Our soul is the owner of the chariot and the one who gets to enjoy the journey. Our mind is the charioteer, and the reins are our five senses, which are represented by five wild horses. Only when the mind works wisely with the wildness of the horses can we run a good race and reach our goal.

You see, there's a part of our brain called the thalamus that treats our inner thoughts, imaginings, and fantasies the same way it treats actual sensory information about the real world. In other words, it makes no distinction between the stories we imagine in our heads, the movies we watch on TV, and outer reality. If you think about and imagine scary things (or watch them on the news or Netflix), your body interprets them as actually happening to you!

This miraculous power means we have the ability to literally create our perceived physiological reality. As Andrew Newberg and Mark Robert Waldman say in their book *Words Can Change Your Brain*, "Our language-based thoughts shape our consciousness, and consciousness shapes the reality we perceive. So choose your words wisely because they become as real as the ground on which you stand."

The ancient teachings also speak of this—and at great length. In fact, much of the *Yoga Sutras* is an original psychology of mind, offering a wellspring of useful instruction on how to use our thoughts, emotions, and senses *wisely*.

According to Ayurveda, the number one way to preserve our vital life force (aka the light that makes us glow!) is to avoid the people, places, and things that disturb our mind.

Practical Ways for Protecting Your Light

▼ **Make morning meditation nonnegotiable.** Before turning on your phone or getting into your daily tasks, take a moment to soak yourself like a little tea bag in some light. It can be as simple as spending two minutes in bed feeling gratitude for what is right in your life flow in your body. It can also be a seated practice that lasts much longer. Pledge a commitment to daily discipline that makes your spiritual light the first thing in your life. I promise, magic will begin to flow the more you make Spirit your #1.

▼ **Avoid "eating" bad stuff.** Part of embodying the protectress of our light is being aware of what we take in on every level. That includes food. When we ingest fast food, we not only get an inflammatory response in our physical body, we also block the healthy flow of our energy. It's like our inner light gets smothered in a layer of Big Macs. Other things we "consume" that, depending on their content, can smother our light include social media, movies, porn, drugs, music, and even what we put on our skin.

▼ **Eat good stuff.** Things that feed our light are the things that are life-giving, life-affirming, and non-addictive. Old-school mystics talked about the sound of water, chirping birds, and the colors of nature. My list includes baby laughter, good books, the birds at sunrise, the sound of the ocean, the magic of sunset, smiles from friends. . . . What's on your list of good stuff?

▼ **Get hip to light and sound.** Pure light and sacred sound are soul medicines that boost our access to our inner light. There are some amazing tools out there that can help you bring more high-vibe light and sound into your body and clear the dust off your own innate light. These can include singing bowls, binaural beats, supersonic brain light, singing songs, chanting mantras, dancing to deep beats, and any other positive, life-affirming light and sound to inspire you. (I've included a list of some of the tech and resources I use almost every day in the resources section.) If you don't want to use anything external, you can just tone your vagus nerve the old-fashioned way by humming or chanting, "Om."

▼ **Learn the sacred walk out.** Back when I was a "good girl," I couldn't imagine walking out on anyone or anything. I used to think it was impolite. Now, I am more than happy to (politely) get up and leave if I get a strong "no" signal. I've left movie theaters when a film felt violent to my spirit. I can also say with great joy that I've walked out on exactly three dates in my life.

Long stories, but let's just say one of those first (and only) dates involved an excessive amount of misogynistic ranting from a man with a messy beard covered in buffalo hot-wing sauce and ranch dressing. Leaving twenty minutes into that hot mess of a date remains one of my favorite "protect your spiritual light" life moments. You are not obliged to endure negativity in the name of politeness.

▼ **Make sacred retreat a part of your year.** There is a reason that countless spiritual seekers, from nuns to shamans to spirit women, left daily life. They did it to protect their light. Now, I am not suggesting that you run off and join a monastery, nor do I think everyone can afford to take expensive yoga vacations to Bali. But making time for sacred retreat offers us room to cultivate our light. Simply block off a few days or even an afternoon on your calendar. Turn off your devices and retreat into your soul. The more silence and screenlessness, the better. This will supercharge your glow.

▼ **Let go of people who don't truly take delight in your light.** One of the toughest lessons of my life was about letting go of relationships that are harmful to my spirit or simply not congruent with the evolution of my heart. You see, I was schooled to think that if you've known someone forever, they had to be in your world forever. Another unhelpful idea in the spiritually inclined mainstream narrative? That when we are spiritual, we should have so much compassion and tolerance that we should be able to effortlessly get along with everyone. Um, no. Every single ancient text I've read that's worth its salt has discussed the vital importance of hanging out with like-minded people. Even the Buddha himself said that there are some people with whom we need to carry a big stick! In other words, not everyone gets to be in your inner soul circle. My life changed when I made the radical decision to politely and lovingly use the phrase, "This isn't a good fit for me anymore," and let go of friends who weren't a haven for my spirit. That doesn't mean kicking out every buddy who triggers you! But it does mean letting go of the people who run on an undercurrent of mistrust, jealousy, or belittlement. Your closest, most intimate relationships shouldn't feed on anxiety, resentment, and codependency.

▼ **Call in support.** We aren't meant to go at this whole light-building affair alone. I have no idea where I would be without my mentor, Cristal Mortensen, who has sat with me in countless therapy sessions; the numerous teachers, podcasts, and books I've learned from; or the friends and family members who have been there to pick up the phone when I called. You need a matrix of support that can hold things down for you when the going gets tough. Then there is what Cristal calls the Big Guns—the infinite forces of the unseen that are always there for us. These are the allies, guides, spirits, avatars, gods, goddesses, and sacred images that come when we call them. How do we know they are there? Everything in this book has been about refining our perception to be able to better feel their presence in addition to our own.

▼ **Use the Holy Pause before speaking and acting.** If I could recommend only one thing to help you protect your light, it would be this. Pause before reacting. Commit to being a good steward of your own feelings and reactions. To the best of your ability, let them digest before engaging. I know it's not always possible or practical, but the more we can pause before reacting, the better. Because as challenging as this can be to do, the earned rewards are great. Responding from a place of greater integration keeps your own energy field intact, and keeps your light from being blown out. Of course, we can't always get it perfect, and sometimes the adequate response is anger or sadness or fear, but there is a difference between an authentic response and a reaction based on the past.

✦ A GLOW-WORTHY MEDITATION ✦
Calling in the Big Guns

One of the most crucial practices in our healing journey is asking for spiritual guidance to be with us. There is a reason why the *Yoga Sutras* list many intricate breathwork practices, meditations, and contemplations only to remind us that these practices may not be needed if we can just surrender our hearts to God.

There are days when it is easy for me to feel my own Divine connection. And there are days when it is really hard and I have to repeat the meditation below over and over again throughout my practice and the day. But the support is always there. Remember, the teachings say that when we take the first step to reach out toward the Divine, the Divine always reaches back.

Here is the basic outline of a simple practice for connection as given to me by Cristal Mortensen. It has really helped me cultivate an even deeper felt-connection to Divine guidance. Feel free to make it your own.

1. *Get energetically grounded (use the practice from page 194 if you need a reminder).*

2. *Feel the head and heart soften. Become open and receptive.*

3. *Ask with full humility and realness for* your *Divine guidance to come.* *"Please come," you can say. "Please be with me here now at this moment. Help me be with myself. Help me be with all the hard stuff in myself and my life. Please be with me here now." Feel its support in the silence of your mind.*

4. *Open your heart again and again to whatever arises. Become receptive to the guidance. Be patient. Have faith.*

WHOLE AND COMPLETE, UNTO HERSELF

Another way we diminish our light is through wanting other people to fill up our light-tank. In other words, raise your hand if you struggle with wanting outside validation (my hand is raised, by the way). In working with thousands of women, I can assure you, you are far from alone. In fact, women have been struggling with wanting permission to be their true selves—and use their voice to express that self—for a really long time.

One of my favorite definitions of the word *yogini* is "she who is whole and complete, unto herself." That is a tall order—but with love, focus, and practice, it is possible to be both deeply interrelated with our loved ones and the world *and* be whole unto ourselves. Our being becomes a refuge. This requires us to have the capacity to contain and digest our own emotional experience—without needing others to change their behavior so we feel okay. It also requires us to witness, with loving compassion, the overt and subtle ways we seek validation from outside sources.

Mythology is rife with stories where women—especially young women—have their validity questioned, often over and over again. The story typically goes something like this:

A young woman sets off on an important journey to fulfill a difficult task. When she gets where she needs to go, inevitably some ugly monster, wayward king, or underworld petty guard halts her in her tracks.

"How dare you!?" they say. "Under *whose* authority do you come here?"

This mythic question is a necessary one. It asks the immature aspect of our womanhood to grow up. To show up for herself. To speak from a place of integrity. To stop waiting on the world to change so we can be okay. And to stop, for the love of all things holy, asking for external permission. You are here by your *own* authority.

Questions of validity may show up in your life as something like these:

Do I have enough qualifications to share my passions and services?

What will my partner/mom/friend think about this?

Can I really wear this outfit?

Will my partner/parent ever change so I can finally feel okay?

Are my opinions aligned with my doctor's/mentor's/political party's opinion?

Just who do I think I am to create that, dream that, call that up?!

Being in our light is all about having a relationship with ourselves. It's about feeling our own energy, power, and presence as a portal that connects us with something bigger than ourselves—something Cosmically Holy. In a sense, all of the methods, practices, and philosophies in this book have been leading us to this moment—to a place where we have built so much presence, love, intuition, energy, integrated shadow, and light that we understand what it is to be whole. To be holy. As these qualities grow, we can know the part of us that is infinitely wise and infinitely kind (even when our transient mood is unpleasant).

This place where we have now arrived is also a tender one, because when we embrace our inner light as the *only* thing that can truly nourish our deepest longing, it means we have to stop the blame game. We understand deeply that we are the only ones who can digest our past. We take full responsibility for our life going forward.

More and more, we realize that our glow comes from our inner light. If we let it, our inner light can guide us and illuminate our steps. Our inner light also may speak to us like a still, small voice. This light has been with us since we took our first breath and will be with us when we take our last. Being in this inner light's guidance is the realm of our spiritual awakening, and is the place where we learn to become the queens of our own lives. More light-power helps us use our God(dess)-given free will to make choices in our lives. We can see if we are living from a place of what we really want, or if someone else's voice is telling us what to do—whether that's our parents or partners, big corporations, the church, government, Instagram. . . . We can begin to see which of our decisions are coming from the whacked-out parts of our culture and which are coming from our courageous hearts. And we can access clarity around these questions only when we have a strong chord of connection to our spiritual practice.

Our inner light is where our true sense of worth comes from. It is a worth that no one can ever destroy. And it is the only kind of power that really matters.

14

Surrender

I t may seem counterintuitive, but one of the greatest ways to step into more and more of our inner light's glow is to surrender to a higher power. We may consider inviting this Higher Source to support us, especially with the most challenging aspects of life. By inviting in a Divine will (as opposed to our personal will alone), we are paradoxically *more* empowered in our personal choices and we grow our light-power exponentially. Through this process, we may see that spiritual power comes from surrendering our old ways into a new vision. So in this chapter, we will take a deeper look at the idea of surrender as a spiritual superpower.

In other words, are you ready to do a spiritual trust fall?

So many of the greatest spiritual experiences and gifts of awakening come from doing the very thing we've been avoiding for a really long time: letting go. This is the nature of surrender. It is deeply counterintuitive to the part of us that wants to keep it all together.

Surrender is about admitting the deepest human truth: We are not in control. And this scares the you-know-what out of us.

But there's good news! On the other side of the pain of this admission is bliss.

When we finally let go of the need for total control and order, we are flushed with an immense sense of relief. When we accept that reality is not black and white . . . that things aren't always fair . . . that the perceived good guys don't always win . . . that death and loss are a part of life . . . when we can really hold these essentials in our hearts, dig our heels in, and commit to keeping our hearts open, we are touching the grace of surrender.

If you are anything like me, sometimes you look around your current life and think, *Wow, this looks absolutely nothing like the hopes and dreams of my younger days.* And even when we get our dreams, the white-picket-fenced houses of our lives inevitably offer us their fair share of front-yard sinkholes. It's almost comical how we fantasize about ideal love and roll over to find our snoring, very human husband. We long for children, and then we're gifted with sleepless nights, endless sick days, and poopy diapers. We land our dream job, but our boss is a tyrant.

This is where surrender comes in. One of the greatest spiritual powers we can cultivate is the capacity to *allow life to be what it is. Allowing, emptiness, receptivity, openness*—these are all words that describe the Divine feminine within us all. And by embracing these qualities, we make friends with what is available to us in the current moment. By resting in a level of acceptance of what *is*, we surrender the inner and outer weapons of war that constantly fight to make our life something different than it is. Of course, this doesn't mean we don't step out of abusive situations or fight injustices or abandon ambition (it's good to have goals!). It just means that we can also accept the reality of a universe that, despite our best efforts, may have its own agenda. In this way, we can find rest outside the ego's need to control outcomes.

As we have discussed throughout the book, one of the reasons we contract ourselves and close down our hearts is that this (temporarily) protects us from the rawness of our experiences. And that's okay. But slowly, as we surrender our lives to what is and we allow for what is unwanted or lacking, a new capacity emerges: trust. Resting in this spiritual superpower, we can handle the intensity of our human, embodied, emotional experience more and more.

Spiritual teachings from all traditions remind us that at least some (if not most) of the pain we experience in life is related not to our current reality, but to past perceptions. By pausing enough to feel our body's raw experience, we can cultivate the open heart we need to surrender.

✳ A GLOW-WORTHY MEDITATION ✳
Opening the Heart

Notice any areas in your life where you may feel yourself contracted and closed off. What feels intolerable? Unfair? Not what you dreamed of? As you bring the things you don't want or you feel are missing into the frame of your attention, notice what starts to happen in your body. Do you feel open to yourself and your life? Or closed off? What emotions arise?

Now invite in presence and openheartedness. What would it feel like in this minute to open your heart to whatever is here? Say to yourself and to the things in your life, "You are allowed to be here." Opening your heart to anger is allowed. Opening your heart to sickness is allowed. Opening your heart to spinning thoughts is allowed. Open your heart to dreams and losses, the messed up relationships, the aches and pains. Just take a moment to allow them all to exist, without trying to make them different. Simply feel your heart meet them with openness.

Continue to open your heart to what is. Notice what begins to change as you keep opening your heart to yourself and your human life. Sense this quality of openhearted surrender. What would it feel like to not be shut down to anything, inside or out?

Can you find a place of quiet witness within the wildness of life? Can you feel the part of you that's always okay, despite the outer world's conditions or the chaos in your mind? Can you feel the part of you that is already surrendered?

GOING DEEPER INTO SURRENDER

Cultivating surrender awakens an inner orientation of *Yes!* to ourselves and the world. Imagine saying yes to whatever is here. Within and without. From that place of open acceptance, we actually have a choice. We can respond to our life (even when that response is a big no) from a place of openness rather than reaction.

Surrender also orients us to our own higher power, our highest mind, and connects us to Divinity. Many religions (and Alcoholics Anonymous!) hold surrender to a higher power as the most important aspect of spiritual life: the willingness to admit that there is an aspect of us that is powerless, and that we need a higher power to take over in our lives.

As you contemplate spiritual surrender, you may be wondering: *What is it that I am surrendering to?*

The answer depends on your very personal and intimate experience. Some of us may relate to this higher aspect as a personal relationship to God or to another holy Christian figure like Jesus or Mary, or to our inner Buddha. For some of us, we need not invoke a Divine force. We sense it as a higher aspect of mind, or the true light of who we are. For others, it is the presence of silence. An emptiness that is full.

As we start to soften our need for controlling outcomes, we will inevitably find that by letting go, we actually open into a deeper, wiser, more expansive version of ourselves. By releasing our tight grip on the way we want things to be, we invite compassionate presence into *what actually is.* We love ourselves and our lives by allowing them to exist, as they are, exactly in their uncomfortable and unwanted forms.

Surrender also allows us to move out of our past and into the possibilities of the future. One of the great gifts of surrender is that the more we let go, the more energetically, mentally, and even physically receptive we become. Receptivity is an openness to the great mystery of *I Don't Know What Will Happen* and, in that, a readiness for whatever comes. It is also, paradoxically, a magnetic force, allowing more of what we do want to come to us, as we stop constantly bracing against what we don't want. Less effort, more flow.

We just jump. Knowing there is no guarantee of a net. But, as one of my favorite meditation teachers, Pema Chödrön, has been known to say, maybe there is no ground below us anyway.

TEN WAYS WE CAN BUILD PRACTICE AROUND SURRENDER

Like everything else in this book, surrendering is easier said than done. And while "top ten ways to . . ." may seem trite when approaching such a nuanced and personal subject as spiritual surrender, there *are* methods that can help you open the door to it. Surrender is a muscle that we can strengthen through practice.

Sometimes surrendering to our lives involves a linear, practical path, moving from one step to another, but more often we can utilize any of the following approaches in tandem. As you read through this list, notice what lights up in your body. What is calling your attention most? What sparks the most inner glow?

1. **Wake up from the trance of control.** One of the first steps in moving toward surrender is waking up from the false idea that we are in total control of our lives. It can be incredibly liberating to notice the subtle and overt ways we are attempting to control ourselves, our lives, and even others. Waking up to the essential pain of *not* being in total control of outcomes can bring more curiosity, openness, and freedom into our lives.

2. **Find silence.** One of the quickest ways to move into spiritual surrender is to quiet the mind. Let go of thinking to the best of your ability. Find the inner witness behind the mind's chatter. Watch the way the mind wiggles and squirms. Witness how it endlessly plots and plans ways of getting more control and avoiding pain. See the thinking mind and ask it to rest. *Be in the quiet.* That silence *is* Divine Surrender.

3. **Get embodied.** Moving our attention out of the ongoing inner narrative and into the raw experience of our body is a theme we've returned to again and again. Surrender is no different. Once we have accepted things as they are on the outside, we can begin to feel things as they are

on the inside. When we let go of resistance to ourselves and our lives, we can feel what we have been running from.

4. **Have faith.** Bringing in an element of faith can open our hearts into surrender. Faith is not unquestioning belief; it is an orientation. Faith invites us into deep questioning: Do you believe that this life has your back? Do you believe that there is a sacred unfolding? That something beyond your limited egoic mind might be enacting a process of soul evolution inside of you? Our intellect may never know the answers to these questions, but orienting our hearts by them can open us into greater surrender. Faith can also be cultivated through gratitude for the life we currently have. We can think of faith as an indwelling heart vibration that holds the position that our life, messy as it is, is deeply worth living. Faith understands that there is a soul-level learning journey taking place.

5. **Forgive others.** In my own life, I have found that one of the fastest ways to deepen my surrender is to forgive others. Forgiveness requires more surrender, and in turn, surrender allows more forgiveness to flow. Continually holding on to old grievances hurts us, stresses out our bodies, and hardens the neurostructures of our brains, making us less open to future possibilities. But we cannot force or rush this process— we must be willing to move through the full range of emotions that can emerge as we open to forgiveness. The key is to remain steadfast in the intention to be free from grievance.

6. **Petition for forgiveness—inside and out.** We may also need to petition for forgiveness from others. There is a reason so many spiritual traditions ask us to take stock of our lives and ask others to forgive us, even those we feel the most aggrieved by (I know, weird, right?). Perhaps, in being forgiven, we can more easily forgive the person we most need to take off the hook of resentment: ourselves. When I struggled despite wanting badly to forgive my perceived enemies, I found that as I practiced being with myself and my feelings, the one I was actually holding resentment toward was *me*.

7. **Bring in the Big Guns**. Again? Yes, again. Ask the Divine to support you in your intention to let go and *allow more*. Call in any angels, allies, ancestors, spirit guides, or gods/goddesses that are meaningful to you to come to your side. If this is too woo-woo for you, no worries. Simply ask the highest aspect of you—your soul—to help you in transforming your thoughts and mind toward the energy of surrender and acceptance, first of self and then of others and all of life. Ask the Divine to allow you to see yourself and others through the eyes of spirit. Be willing to see your life in a new, surrendered way. Return to the previous meditations in this book for support.

8. **Get out of the past.** Surrender involves being willing to submit our thoughts of past pain to the fire of what a brighter, more loving future holds. And despite how wonderful surrender may sound, trying to force it is like trying to force digestion. Like forgiveness, you can't *force* letting go. You must sit back, hold within you the intention of opening your heart, and patiently wait for the process to unfold. Replaying past offenses over and over again in your mind is normal, but it is also an impediment to the clearer vision that surrendering those thoughts can bring.

9. **Serve others.** A surrendered life can be deeply augmented by intentionally moving out of our own plans and desires. While there is absolutely nothing wrong with having plans and desires, a counterbalance to these impulses of the ego are acts of selfless service. Volunteering is a great place to move our energy. When we start serving other people and holding an intention to be a vessel for something bigger than ourselves, life has a magical way of serving us back.

10. **Be patient.** Trust that, just like giving birth, deepening surrender takes time and effort. It is usually uncomfortable and painful. It often involves way more than saying a prayer, chanting a mantra, or doing a cool cord-cutting ceremony to release all your terrible exes. Those things can help, but having a surrendered, open heart is a lifestyle, not a one-off experience. It involves a serious commitment to accepting

your life as it is and to loving even the parts about it that feel like the worst. This level of love and surrender is not for the weak, my friend, but it is a sure sign of the very brave.

SAYING YES TO LIFE

Ultimately, surrender is about being open to your life. Loving it without having to like it. As it is. Mess and all. When we say yes, we stay open. We stay ready to be surprised. We become supple instead of contracted.

It is important to remember that saying yes to ourselves, our lives, and this world (which at times seems so out of whack) does not mean we can't also say no. But within our healthy boundaries, our to-do lists and disciplines, we retain a greater openness of mind that is *allowing* it all. In other words, even a *No* can exist within a cosmic *Yes!*

When we are in the small mind of the ego, we can't see our heart's true longing. In fact, the more we surrender to our lives as they are now, the more we allow for the clarity to see the deepest dreams and longings of our hearts. Cultivating more awareness and love, as we've done throughout this book, in turn serves to clarify the mind and interpret the quiet truths of the heart.

✳ A GLOW-WORTHY CONTEMPLATION ✳
Loosening the Grip of Control

Where are the areas in my life where I must maintain control?

What is hardest for me to let go of and surrender?

*What would it feel like if I didn't judge myself or
reality about its worth as good or bad?*

*What if I was already worthy and my life was
worthy exactly as it is, warts and all?*

What aspects of my life and myself am I holding a resistance toward?

What areas of my life and myself do I find intolerable?

What would my life look like if I never got my dream job, mate, child, home, wealth, etc.? How can I keep my heart open to this possibility?

What would it feel like in my mind and my body if I just accepted myself and my life right now?

SURRENDER ALLOWS THE EMOTIONS TO COME

As we practice surrender, we may initially find it to be a very emotional experience. When we loosen the grips of control, we may need to grieve for the life we wanted but currently do not have. Letting go may bring up the sadness of loss as we release strong attachments to our past or our future. It might mean surrendering to the fact that we *didn't* get the dream job, or we *aren't* married to the love of our life, or we're *still* struggling with the same chronic health issues or addictions.

Perhaps the *Bhagavad Gita* said it best. In it, Krishna (who is a representation of our higher self, or God) says to Arjuna (a representation of our more limited self), "Abandon all varieties of Dharma [purpose] and simply surrender unto Me alone. I shall liberate you from all sinful [ignorant] reactions. Do not fear."

As we continue to surrender into reality as it is, we become liberated, and we begin to have a deeper relationship with life. More and more, we can exist in the starkness of the present moment *unapologetically*. We are with the wild pulse of life's continual rawness. We can sense the deep spiritual truth of all of us: There is nothing to hold on to. Everything is a wave of temporality and impermanence. We can taste the shakiness of our tender humanity. We can feel the vulnerability in the fundamental groundlessness of our lives, and how we may have structured our thoughts and routines around avoiding feeling this deepest of life's lessons.

As we practice and cultivate our ability to experience greater and greater levels of intensity—whether of emotions, vibrations, thoughts, images, or primal sensations in our bodies—this very fact of our fundamental openness can often lead to a deeper experience of freedom.

A GLOW-WORTHY MEDITATION
The Golden Egg

Just surrender. It's so easy to say and so hard to do! The following meditation has its origins in the Tantric idea that you exist and are held within a perfect, luminous, golden egg of protective, nurturing energy. Some call it the auric field.

Take a moment to remind yourself that you
deserve to take a pause in your life.

You deserve to relax into your own presence, no matter what state you find
yourself in. No matter what is going on in the outer world. You deserve
to fill up with and feel the belonging and safety that is your birthright. It
doesn't come from the outside world, but from within you, holding you.

Start to feel the contact between your body and the chair or floor.

Feel the weight of your body, gravity like a gift, pulling
you down into this moment. Here and now.

Attune to your breath. Notice the rise and fall of the inhale and exhale.

Feel the gentle pause at the top of the inhale and bottom of the exhale.

Follow every millimeter of the breath. As if it mattered. As if it were enough.

As you relax more and more deeply into accepting every
aspect of this moment, inner and outer, say to yourself, silently
or aloud: I am held in a soft membrane, a perfect golden
egg. It can nurture and fill me. Hold and protect me.

Let your eyes soften and become even more
receptive. I am here. And I am held.

Let your heart soften and become even more
receptive. I am here. And I am held.

Let your belly soften and become even more
receptive. I am here. And I am held.

Now be present with the stream of thoughts or images in your mind. Try
not to judge any thoughts bad or wrong. Just be with them. Let your mind
soften and become even more receptive. I am here. And I am held.

Notice any feelings, moods, or emotions you are experiencing.
Without labeling them as bad or good, simply notice them. Notice
also how both the thoughts and emotions shift and change. Notice
how it all shifts and changes. Let your emotional being soften
and become even more receptive. I am here. And I am held.

Feel this presence more and more like an egg all around you.

Feel, sense, or just imagine that you are sitting inside this beautiful
textured egg. Imagine it like an energy-filled cellular membrane all around
your physical body. Feel the edges of this soft, permeable egg. Imagine
its curvature as smooth and strong. This boundary of personal energy is
intelligent. It knows what to let in and what to keep out. Feel and intuit
any areas of this personal energy egg that may feel torn or loose. Perhaps
there is more energy in front of you than behind you. Pour your attention
into the parts of the egg where you cannot clearly sense the boundary.

For me, it's helpful to imagine someone pouring golden-pink
honey about a foot above my head. The honey forms the boundary
of the egg all around me, six or maybe 12 inches away from
my physical body. You can use any imagery that works.

Now, feel energy and your attention moving up from the earth,
filling your physical body and expanding all around you within the
boundary of this cosmic, protective, nourishing egg. Keep filling
up again, over and over, until the whole field around you holds a
texture. This may be challenging at first, but the more you practice,
the more you will feel the energy is working on its own. Rather
than you moving it around, it begins to move and teach you.

Feel held in this egg. Know that it is ancient and forever new. It's been with you since the moment you took your first breath, and it will go with you at the moment of death. Rest in this presence, remembering that mantra: I am here. And I am held.

SURRENDERING OUR EGO BRINGS OPENINGS

First things first: There is nothing wrong with having an ego. In fact, in order to show up in the world, create good boundaries, and have self-esteem, we need to have a solid sense of our individuality. It's an intrinsic part of our psychological makeup. But our ego—the ongoing inner dialogue that feels separate, works for its own good, and lives in a very limited reality—can also wreak havoc on our life. This occurs when we identify this part of our psychology as the *totality* of who we are—when we confuse who we are with the ego's narrative of personality, identities, hopes, desires, fears, manipulations, and defense mechanisms.

There is one particular quality of ego that is its ultimate wall of defense: separation. When we feel that we are separate from nature, God, and others, other emotional states ensue. When we feel isolated, we feel vulnerable, and often wall ourselves off in an attempt to protect ourselves. But this only leads us to feel more isolated. This sense of vulnerability may also lead us to double down on our defenses (fight/flight) and our manipulations (control).

I definitely have an ego. My ego thinks she is a big, tall blonde with a sensitive heart and a big mouth (literally and figuratively). She is also very soft and feminine, and loving to a fault. She is as pious as she is profane. She is as prone to self-righteousness as she is illumination and compassion. She is goofy, romantic, slovenly, sexy, smart, dumb, and sometimes petty and obsessive. She has an amazing longing for light and a healthy awareness of her dark side.

What is your ego like?

Our egos often tell us a particularly juicy lie: "You can get more of what you want and always avoid what you don't." But as the Buddha summed up nicely with this core message of his spiritual path: Attachment and aversion are the roots of our suffering.

This is where surrender can open our minds to something bigger than our small, egoic perceptions. As we open to life as it is, without trying to control, fix, or even attain, our sense of separation from the world begins to dissolve, and something like freedom can take its place. The more we let go, the more an infinite divine radiance can fill us with its presence. In other words, the deeper the surrender, the more space we create for the glow of our inner light.

As we stay centered in the uncertainty of our lives, we begin to tap into deeper layers of truth. We gain a sense of confidence and compassion that comes from knowing our interrelatedness with all living things. Our bodies and minds become more capacious, able to hold more light, and we become more spiritually alive. We become more and more willing to be what we have always been: glow-worthy.

We all know that some of our greatest spiritual awakenings come from moments when our lives are a veritable train wreck. This has been painfully true for me, and I've heard similar stories from the thousands of women in our school. They have told me of their own greatest losses—illness, divorce, abuse, the loss of a loved one, a heart attack, and other very tender human experiences—and, often, about how on the other side of that pain was a deep lesson. And for that lesson, they were grateful.

This is not to take away from how much life can challenge us. We shouldn't rush to candy-coat our histories in the glitter of a spiritual lesson. (Remember spiritual bypassing?) That said, the greatest moments of bliss in our spiritual lives often do not come when we are having orgasms, eating bonbons, and playing with puppies (although it's possible, I'm sure!). No, they come from having surrendered to the depths of pain and loss and emerged, a little more glowing, on the other side.

By being willing to die a little bit every single day, we surrender into rebirth. By shedding the old skin of our past perceptions, desires, and avoidances, we can be made anew. Like a chubby, innocent baby, we are full of youthful light, no matter our age. We glow not because we are perfect, but because we are real.

15

Holy, Happy Endings:
A Love Letter to You

Dear Reader,

I feel like we've gone on a journey together, even though I can't see you, nor you me.

But here I am, writing these words cross-legged, hair in a messy bun, drinking a green tea way too late in the day, thinking about you. And me. And my longing for all of us, especially women, to truly know our holiness.

Maybe this book will sit on your nightstand, never to be read, but magically absorbed as if through osmosis.

Maybe it will be covered in hot pink highlighter and returned to often.

Maybe you will buy a copy for your mom or your friend.

Maybe there are words in here that make you cry.

Maybe you will throw this book across the room because it pisses you off.

No matter what, I hope that there is something inside these pages that inspires you toward more light.

This is my heart's true longing: that we, together, can walk each other home.

And here's the thing. *You can't be a part-time light worker.* Being a truly holy human, in the fullest sense of the word, means being a full-timer.

Don't get me wrong, I know from personal experience that this journey toward our union with the Divine within is a messy one. Some days I feel like I'm pushing a spiritual rock up a steep mountain, connecting with my inner trust, radiance, and light, only to be flung back as I revisit my old, painful ways—the ones I am embarrassed to admit I still struggle with.

But being a full-time light worker has nothing to do with having an easy journey. Being a full-time light worker means taking a vow to make living an authentic, spiritual life the greatest goal in your life.

And so, as we close these pages, I have one last question for you: Are you in?

THE LAST SECRET

No matter how great this (or any) book is, it can never take you to the sublime. Any moments of sparkly joy you may have had while reading this *are coming from inside you.*

You see, no forty-day program, mind-blowing festival, or breathwork technique—or even the best teacher in the world—can take you to the sacred realm of the numinous. The best these things can do is catalyze a melting process. Remove a veil. Point to the moon.

Before this book, you were *already* glow-worthy. Always have been. Always will be. And as I finish writing the pages of this book, I realize that I wrote it as much for me as I did for you. Because I need a manual and a reminder as much as the next gal.

There is a beautiful word in Sanskrit that speaks to this re-remembering of our inner divinity: *smarana,* or "remembrance." The best a book like this can do is help reveal the thing we all forget: that we are loved. Deeply.

The last secret is that how much you yearn for love is exactly equal to the force of life that is just waiting to love you in return. You just have to be open to letting it in.

GO FOR THE GOLD, NOT JUST WORMS

Throughout this book, I've tried to remind you that your relationship to the sacred doesn't need to be passed through the lens of any one individual, culture, or even religious tradition. You hold—through your body, mind, and spirit—a direct line of communication to the realm of holiness. And the holiness that is inside you is in *all* things. It weaves through us all, ever-present and steady, like a protective, loving friend. So often we turn to things outside ourselves, thinking they will hold the keys to our holiness, forgetting that we hold a glowing mystical medicine inside our own heart.

I have one last holy story for you. I can't remember the origin, but I want to tell it in my own words as best I can. It goes something like this:

Inside your heart exist two doves. The first of these doves is always hungry, and leaves the nest, ignoring the second, golden dove beside her. She flits and flies about looking for a worm to quell her hunger. Sometimes she finds a worm and feels a temporary glimmer of happiness. But she always becomes hungry again. And the search for more worms begins once more.

Eventually, the little dove becomes exhausted. She returns home to her nest, where the other dove—infinitely kind and infinitely wise—sits patiently awaiting her. As she returns home to her nest, she is filled to the brim with the gaze of the golden dove. She is filled with a nourishing nectar that knows no bounds and is in endless supply.

You would think that upon tasting this inner nectar, the little dove would never leave the nest again. But she forgets. And she flies off again looking for worms. But one day, she doesn't forget, and although she may still enjoy flying and hunting worms, she knows that true nourishment means returning home to her golden sister.

This story is a story about you. About us. About forgetting and remembering. About our flight away from our truest self, and our eventual return.

I hope, with all my heart, we all find the gold: that real glow that was ours by birthright all along.

Katie

RESOURCES AND FURTHER READING

FOR AYURVEDA, TANTRA, AND WOMEN-CENTERED HEALTH COACHING

Shakti Ayurveda School

Shakti Ayurveda School's level 1 training is a 300-hour, yearlong deep dive into my signature Divine Feminine Ayurveda teachings, weaving in our faculty's varied backgrounds in functional medicine, psychology, neuroscience, and more. This course is for heart-centered souls who want to expand their understanding of healing, women's wisdom traditions, and holistic medicine. It's based on the idea that it's possible to experience abundant health, passion, and vitality at any age, and eliminate the divide between spiritual and worldly fulfillment.

Connect here for more info: https://theshaktischool.com/ayurveda -school/

Spirit Sessions Subscription

The Shakti School's mission is to uplift and nurture feminine-form movement and healing arts, and to support women stepping into their spiritual and creative authority.

Connect here to subscribe to our members-only portal: https://theshakti school.com/subscribe/

Spirit Sessions Podcast

Spirit Sessions is your one-stop shop for all things emergent in sex, spirituality, and self-care. Join me for the best of science, ancient holistic medicine, and spiritual up-leveling. This podcast is full of fun and deep real-talk from your fave Ayurveda gal Friday on holistic health, femme-form biohacking, mysticism, and anything else that makes your life a better place to live. Mostly, this podcast is personal. It's me speaking my most authentic heart. No holds barred. No fear. Just me, you, rad guests, and soulful convo.

https://theshaktischool.com/podcast/

FOR CEREMONY WORK

Mer Hogan, *The Beauty Way*
https://thebeautyway.net

FOR SOMATICS, TRAUMA, AND ATTACHMENT WORK

Cristal Mortensen, *Aware Aligned Awake*
https://awarealignedawake.com

Vanessa Durrant, *Kindred Tree Healing Center*
https://kindredtreehealing.com/vanessa-durrant

Havening Trauma Release
https://traumathrivers.com/havening/

Somatic Experiencing International
https://traumahealing.org

Hakomi Institute
https://hakomiinstitute.com

FOR ENERGY WORK

Cristal Mortensen, *Aware Aligned Awake*
https://awarealignedawake.com

Rosalyn Bruyere
https://rosalynlbruyere.org

FOR STRESS HEALING WITH SOUND, LIGHT, AND BREATHWORK

BrainTap
https://braintap.com

Othership
https://www.othership.us/app

Apollo
https://apolloneuro.com

Sensate
https://buy.getsensate.com/hero-story/

FOR DEVELOPMENTAL PSYCHOLOGY AND AWARENESS

Dr. Dan Siegel
https://drdansiegel.com

FOR SEX AND RELATIONSHIP COUNSELING

Barbara Gabriel, *Love & Marriage Works*
https://loveandmarriageworks.com

Chris Muse
https://chris-muse.com

MENTAL HEALTHCARE FOR MARGINALIZED COMMUNITIES

Ayana Therapy
https://ayanatherapy.com

The Loveland Foundation
https://thelovelandfoundation.org

MORE BOOKS AND RESOURCES

There are many books that could act as supplemental reading on the concepts explored in this book. I've listed some of my favorite recommendations on trauma, healing, female sexuality, yoga and Tantra, and other topics at this link for easy access: https://theshaktischool .com/books-we-love/

ACKNOWLEDGMENTS

To my parents, Vera and Larry Silcox, for raising me to value humor, authenticity, and a sincere connection to God.

To my brother, Wyatt, who shows me every day what selfless service looks like. To my sister, Mary, who is my constant companion on this walk toward Buddha-hood. And to Mary K. and Will—I love you guys.

I must also bow to the constant sources of ecstatic fun and effortless love in my life, Jack Walker Silcox (previously known as "Baby Jack") and my goddaughter, Clara Silcox. I hope you both read this book one day and can always feel my love and support.

I also want to deeply thank my friend and mentor Cristal Mortensen. The experiences we have shared and the wisdom you hold are woven throughout so much of this book. Thank you for being a source of constancy, trust, and love, both tender and fierce. You have taught me how to truly *be* with all of myself and to tune in to the unseen light that was with me all along. I love that you can lead us toward enlightenment while also surfing, drinking coffee, and cracking up like an '80s teenager at an Air Space concert.

To Mer Hogan, for being my precious friend and spiritual sidekick. You, your laughter, and your spirit are such a healing force in my life and this world. It's awesome when your best friends are also your best teachers. Thank you for your contributions to this book and the world.

To Kirstin Mackey, MD, for all the courageous healing work you do, for being a great friend, and for taking my SOS "Help me!" texts throughout the writing of this book. Your knowledge and insight into the inner workings of physiology and the beauty of how conscious osteopathic medicine can blend into Ayurveda and the philosophy of Tantra is of such value to this world and The Shakti School. Thank you for being one of the bravest and most honest docs on the planet right now.

To Kelle Walsh, the original editor of this book (and many previous versions). Thank you for always "getting it," and for your commitment to truth in writing. You were more than an editor—you were a wise friend.

To Chad Harbach, for giving great literary and health/life/love advice. And for teaching me that I could write how I speak and that would be enough.

To Liz Reynolds, for reading parts of this book and crying real tears. Thank you for our grounded friendship. I value you so much. You are one of the reasons this book is here.

To Faith Levine, for helping me trust my body and being a guide of the heart.

To Janis and John Humphries, for being my favorite surrogate aunt and uncle and for supporting me on so many levels. Janis, thank you for being The Shakti School's "Julia Sugarbaker of Human Resources." And John, thanks for always being ready to get the snakes out.

To Sarah Waldron, the director of The Shakti School, for being such an amazing manager and caring force for all the students in our program. Your loving pit bull nature is a stable force for me and our community. You are truly a priceless gem in my life.

To my agent, Dana Newman, for believing in the project. I'm really grateful that you "got it" from the beginning.

To all of the team at BenBella, in particular: Leah Wilson, Leah Baxter, Lindsay Marshall, Karen Wise, Sarah Avinger, Brigid Pearson, Kim Broderick, Adrienne Lang, Susan Welte, Alicia Kania, Madeline Grigg, Raquel Moreno, and Amy Preston.

To the support of: Kiersten Massey, Donna Hodges, Michael Fishman, Tim Highnam, Amy Stanton, Dana Lewis, Belen Castillo, Chalena Cadenas, Denege Prudhomme, Amy Crumpton, Daniela Cisneros, Alicia Farjado, Barbara Gabriel, Mary Thompson, Myra Lewin, Pema Leigh, Ragaia Belovarac, Faith Bendt, and Ojas (aka Butter, aka Missy Elliot).

To all of the teachers and coaches at The Shakti School: Sandhiya Ramaswamy, Dr. Siva Mohan, Meredith Klein, Indu Arora, Laurel Odom, Nidhi Pandya, Tracee Stanley, Brooke Sullivan, Chris Muse, Vanessa Durrant, Dr. Nicole Beurkens, Marissa Angeletti, Ashlee Sakaishi Wilkin, Lisa Marie Rankin, Deborah Bagg, Eva Peterson, Jaclyn DeConti, Dominique Lynch, Laurie Riley, Natalie Wegenka, TaKisha August Adams, and Malia Wright.

And lastly, to the thousands of women I have had the honor of working with at The Shakti School. You are so much more than students in our school; you are kindred spirits. You continually show me that the world is filled with heart-centered people who long for truth and spiritual evolution.

BIBLIOGRAPHY

Aftab, Awais, Ellen E. Lee, Federica Klaus, Rebecca Daly, Tsung-Chin Wu, Xin Tu, Steven Huege, and Dilip V. Jeste. "Meaning in Life and Its Relationship with Physical, Mental, and Cognitive Functioning: A Study of 1,042 Community-Dwelling Adults across the Lifespan." *Journal of Clinical Psychiatry* 81, no. 1 (2019): 11357.

Allione, Tsultrim. *Feeding Your Demons: Ancient Wisdom for Resolving Inner Conflict.* Boston: Little, Brown Spark, 2008.

Anderson, James W., and Paige A. Nunnelley. "Private Prayer Associations with Depression, Anxiety, and Other Health Conditions: An Analytical Review of Clinical Studies." *Postgraduate Medicine* 128, no. 7 (2016): 635–41.

Bachman, Nicolai. *The Path of the Yoga Sutras: A Practical Guide to the Core of Yoga.* Sounds True, 2011.

Benson, Kyle. "The Magic Relationship Ratio, According to Science." Gottman Institute. May 13, 2021. https://www.gottman.com/blog/the-magic -relationship-ratio-according-science/.

Boelens, Peter A., Roy R. Reeves, William H. Replogle, and Harold G. Koenig. "The Effect of Prayer on Depression and Anxiety: Maintenance of Positive Influence One Year after Prayer Intervention." *International Journal of Psychiatry in Medicine* 43, no. 1 (2012): 85–98.

Brosowsky, Nicholaus P., Nathaniel Barr, Jhotisha Mugon, Abigail A. Scholer, Paul Seli, and James Danckert. "Creativity, Boredom Proneness and Well-Being in the Pandemic." *Behavioral Sciences* 12, no. 3 (2022): 68.

Cherry, Kendra. "What Is the Negativity Bias?" Verywell Mind, April 29, 2020. https://www.verywellmind.com/negative-bias-4589618.

Chowdhury, Madhuleena Roy. "The Neuroscience of Gratitude and How It Affects Anxiety and Grief." PositivePsychology.com, February 5, 2022.

Clift, Stephen, and Ian Morrison. "Group Singing Fosters Mental Health and Wellbeing: Findings from the East Kent 'Singing for Health' Network Project." *Mental Health and Social Inclusion* 15, no. 2 (2011): 88–97.

Crego, Antonio, José R. Yela, María Á. Gómez-Martínez, Pablo Riesco-Matías, and Cristina Petisco-Rodríguez. "Relationships between Mindfulness, Purpose in Life, Happiness, Anxiety, and Depression: Testing a Mediation Model in a Sample of Women." *International Journal of Environmental Research and Public Health* 18, no. 3 (2021): 925.

Easwaran, Eknath, translator. *The Bhagavad Gita*. Nilgiri Press, 2007.

Ellis, Robert J., and Julian F. Thayer. "Music and Autonomic Nervous System (Dys)function." *Music Perception* 27, no. 4 (2010): 317–26.

Exton, Michael S., Tillmann H. C. Kruger, Norbert Bursch, Philip Haake, Wolfram Knapp, Manfred Schedlowski, and Uwe Hartmann. "Endocrine Response to Masturbation-Induced Orgasm in Healthy Men Following a 3-week Sexual Abstinence." *World Journal of Urology* 19, no. 5 (2001): 377–82.

Frankl, Viktor E. *Man's Search for Meaning*. Boston: Beacon Press, 2006.

Gray, John. *Beyond Mars and Venus*. Dallas, TX: BenBella Books, 2017.

Hofmann, Stefan G., Paul Grossman, and Devon E. Hinton. "Loving-Kindness and Compassion Meditation: Potential for Psychological Interventions." *Clinical Psychology Review* 31, no. 7 (2011): 1126–32.

"How to Stimulate Your Vagus Nerve for Better Mental Health." January 17, 2017. https://sass.uottawa.ca/sites/sass.uottawa.ca/files/how_to_stimulate _your_vagus_nerve_for_better_mental_health_1.pdf.

Ishak, Waguih William, Maria Kahloon, and Hala Fakhry. "Oxytocin Role in Enhancing Well-Being: A Literature Review." *Journal of Affective Disorders* 130, no. 1–2 (2011): 1–9.

Jung, C. G., *Psychological Types*. Edited by R. F. C. Hull, translated by H. G. Baynes. London: Princeton University Press, 1990.

Kierkegaard, Søren, *Works of Love*. New York, NY: Harper Perennial Modern Thought, 2009.

Lacey, Beatrice C., and John I. Lacey. "Two-Way Communication between the Heart and the Brain: Significance of Time within the Cardiac Cycle." *American Psychologist* 33, no. 2 (1978): 99.

Lad, Vasant. *Textbook of Ayurveda, Vol. 1: Fundamental Principles of Ayurveda*. Asheville, NC: Ayurvedic Press, 2001.

Love, Tiffany M. "Oxytocin, Motivation, and the Role of Dopamine." *Pharmacology Biochemistry and Behavior* 119 (2014): 49–60.

Lyubomirsky, Sonja. *The How of Happiness: A New Approach to Getting the Life You Want*. New York, NY: Penguin, 2008.

McGilchrist, Iain. *The Master and His Emissary: The Divided Brain and the Making of the Western World*. New Haven, CT: Yale University Press, 2019.

Newberg, Andrew, and Mark Robert Waldman, *Words Can Change Your Brain: 12 Conversation Strategies to Build Trust, Resolve Conflict, and Increase Intimacy*. New York, NY: Plume, 2012.

Nhat Hanh, Thich. *How to Love*. Berkeley, CA: Parallax Press, 2015.

Nhat Hanh, Thich, "Remembering Thich Nhat Hanh, Brother Thay." Interview by Krista Tippett. On Being, January 27, 2022. https://onbeing.org /programs/remembering-thich-nhat-hanh-brother-thay/.

Nhat Hanh, Thich. "This Is the Buddha's Love." Interview by Melvin McLeod. Plum Village, October 5, 2019. https://plumvillage.org/about/thich-nhat -hanh/interviews-with-thich-nhat-hanh/shambhala-sun-march-2006 -exclusive-interview/.

Pirkhaefi, Alireza. "The Effectiveness of Clinical Creativity Therapy Model on Promotion of Executive Functions and Decrease Depression of the Depressed Patients." *Neuropsychology* 4, no. 15 (2019): 21–40.

Rumi, Suhaib. *Emerald Companions*. Independently Published, 2019.

Simão, Talita Prado, Sílvia Caldeira, and Emilia Campos De Carvalho. "The Effect of Prayer on Patients' Health: Systematic Literature Review." *Religions* 7, no. 1 (2016): 11.

Svoboda, Robert. *Aghora, at the Left Hand of God*. Las Vegas, NV: Brotherhood of Life, 2007.

Wolynn, Mark. *It Didn't Start with You: How Inherited Family Trauma Shapes Who We Are and How to End the Cycle.* New York, NY: Penguin, 2017.

Woodman, Marion, *Addiction to Perfection: The Still Unravished Bride.* Toronto: Inner City Books, 1982.

ABOUT THE AUTHOR

Katie Silcox, MAS, AHP, is the *New York Times* bestselling author of the book *Healthy, Happy, Sexy: Ayurveda Wisdom for Modern Women*. Holding a master's degree in Ayurvedic philosophy, she is the founder of The Shakti School, a premier online holistic coaching certification school for women. Her platform focuses on the convergence of ancient medicine, modern science, and heart-centered spirituality. In her former lives, she's been a researcher in artificial intelligence, a cover model for *Yoga Journal* magazine in Russia, and the owner of a beach bar in Spain. She is currently pursuing scholarly work in Jungian psychology, dreamwork, and depth ritual. You can find out more about her at www.katiesilcox .com and www.theshaktischool .com, and by following her on Instagram @theshaktischool.